Praise for
The 20-Minute Networking Meeting

"Couldn't put the book down once I'd started..."

"...has become my bible for networking..."

"What a life SAVING book—a must read for everyone. Simple and brief, but very profound."

"...I strongly recommend this book to anyone, whether they are just starting their career, established in their career, stay-at-home parent, in job transition, volunteer, or re-entering the workforce..."

"Has risen to my top five best business books..."

"Required reading for everyone... Essential for any job seeker."

"Know *exactly* what to do during a networking meeting..."

"...amazed by the results..."

"... not until I read this book did I realize that there was a better and more effective process to networking..."

"...the power of this book lies in helping the reader understand the meeting from the other person's perspective..."

"...places great emphasis on concern for others, and reminds us that etiquette and preparation are important for every successful career move..."

"Navigate around the HR nightmare and secure interviews..."

"...shares actual dialogue of how a meeting or situation may sound..."

"...great tools to use prior to your meeting. An excellent resource..."

"Amidst the myriad of development books on the market, this rises to the top..."

"...I was asked to meet for coffee and the meeting was a slap-in-the-face wake-up moment. The meeting was playing out just as described in the book..."

"A timely wake-up call for anyone trying to network more effectively."

"...valuable insights for honing your networking skills..."

"...intuitive and terrific at illustrating what effective networking is..."

"...I have read several networking books in my career, none of them have put it as succinctly as this..."

"...the beauty of this book is that it provides clear structure to enable even the most introverted person, but also helps the extrovert focus on a respectful and positive use of time..."

"...a must read for anyone in business development..."

"...I have insisted that my human capital consulting Sales/Accounting Managers read the book..."

"...cuts through the rhetoric and gives step-by-step straight forward advice..."

"...outstanding read with straightforward and practical framework that everyone can utilize no matter what career stage..."

"...spells it out in a simple and understandable manner. A quick read and easy to reference..."

"...the lucid and fun writing style made it easy and enjoyable to read cover to cover quickly..."

"...I found myself actually thinking, speaking and behaving

differently with my networking contacts. My conversations simply became much more effective..."

"...this book provides a solid framework and practical advice that anyone—seasoned or just starting out—can use to become more proficient in their networking..."

"...a simple and easy read that will have you smacking your head and saying, 'now why haven't I been doing this?'"

"...easy read, well organized, and has a very logical flow. I would recommend it to everyone, even those who have been networking for a period of time..."

"...networking made EASY!"

"...practical, concise and very well written..."

"...I would recommend this book to anyone, job seeker or not..."

"...*The 20 Minute Networking Meeting* will change the way I network. It also changes the way I present to others, interact with business leaders, and prioritize my time..."

"...prepares you for your meeting, gives you the right questions to ask, as well as lets you know the questions *not* to ask!"

"...A must read for confident and successful networking..."

"...a pithy roadmap for successful conversations during a job search..."

"...just finished and it is spectacular..."

"...a tremendous resource..."

"...a real breakthrough..."

"...by far the best networking guide I've found..."

THE 20-MINUTE NETWORKING MEETING

Professional Edition

WINNER: International Book Awards - Business: Careers
WINNER: National Indie Excellence Award - Careers Category

ALSO BY NATHAN A. PEREZ AND MARCIA BALLINGER

The 20-Minute Networking Meeting, Graduate Edition

The 20-Minute Networking Meeting, Executive Edition

The 20-Minute Networking Meeting

PROFESSIONAL EDITION

Learn to Network. Get a Job.

NATHAN A. PEREZ
and MARCIA BALLINGER, PhD

CAREER INNOVATIONS PRESS

**Non-Profit and Education volume book orders are available at a discount.
Contact Career Innovations Press for more information.
www.20mnm.com**

Published 2016 by Career Innovations Press.
Cover design by Linda Koutsky
Interior design by Linda Koutsky

ISBN-10:0-9859106-4-X

ISBN-13:978-0-9859106-4-8

Marcia would like to dedicate this book to:
her husband, Brad; her daughter Analisa;
and her mother, June.

* * *

Nathan would like to dedicate this book to his mom, Delilah
Naomi Duran, whose undying, unconditional support of all things
creative and business led to the creation of
The 20-Minute Networking Meeting series.
And
To his late father, Seferino Sanchez Perez, who demonstrated that
hard work comes in many forms and always leads to success.

Contents

Acknowledgments

The 20-Minute Networking Meeting is rooted in two core values: Collaboration and Community. We believe that a successful organization (and a successful individual!) needs to care about a wide variety of constituencies and stakeholders and to treat each with concern and respect.

One way that Collaboration and Community come into play is in the networking we, as recruitment professionals, do with people in job transition. Even when we are not working on a related search, we seek to assist each person who contacts us by sharing information with them, offering helpful suggestions, or perhaps, giving a word of encouragement.

Of course, a book like this that stresses the importance of relationships could not be possible without the help, insight, and contributions of others. We would like to acknowledge the wisdom and generosity of a few friends and colleagues from the executive search industry who offered their own networking stories. In particular, we'd like to recognize David Magy and Carla Anderson.

Many business professionals provided their own job-search perspectives on *what it is like out there* and took the time to meet and share their experiences with us. Thank you to Wendy Brauchler; Brad Ballinger; Tom Colosimo; and Jessica Ann Perez.

A special thanks to Mac Prichard and Mac's List in Portland, Oregon; Santiago Strasser; Robert Harrold; and Linda Koutsky for her beautiful book design;

A phenomenal group of organizations and individuals from the career transition industry have also been especially supportive and helpful to us. We'd specifically like to recognize Cultivating Careers; George Dow Consulting; Jane Salmen and Human Capital Partners; Barb Adams at Executive Coaching Insight; Navigate/Forward; Lee Hecht Harrison; Right Management; Challenger; Gray & Christmas; and Beth Glassman. Our heartfelt thanks.

Finally, we owe a debt of gratitude to our editor, Stuart Perelmuter, who always made himself available for the *20MNM* project through its first, second and third incarnations. Thank you, friend.

PART I

Introduction

(Or: Read Me So The Book Makes Sense)

Welcome to *The 20-Minute Networking Meeting!* The information contained in this book *will* revolutionize the way you think about networking, whether you're looking for a job or to proactively manage your career. Meeting with jobseekers every day, we've observed what works in networking—from the hiring side of the desk. Consequently, we've also observed what does *not* work, and sadly, the vast majority of networking meetings are near-complete failures. *The 20-Minute Networking Meeting* is meant to remedy that and to help you develop the most important skill set in business.

Our objective in writing *The 20-Minute Networking Meeting* is to show you what networking looks like from your contacts' perspectives. Following its lessons and advice, you will learn to conduct meetings that those contacts find valuable, engaging, and impressive—all inside twenty minutes. Written by two career professionals with a combined networking experience of over 40 years, the material in this book is designed with *you* in mind. *Everything* in it is relevant to your situation as a jobseeker—even if your networking skills or professional experience is limited.

Based on the same networking model as the acclaimed *Executive Edition,* the *Professional Edition* includes the stories and perspectives of career experts, hiring professionals, and business executives from across a diverse set of industries. The inclusion of such professional experiences are meant to not only give you insight into what to expect during your networking journeys, but with their shared perspectives, teach you how to prepare for it *now*.

So don't skip ahead. Having a full understanding of the *20MNM* model is imperative to your job-seeking success. Mastering it will affect far more than just getting your first or next job. It will impact the rest of your career.

Let's get on with it.

A Couple of
Networking Stories...

Margret & Andy

Margret looked at her calendar. Back-to-back meetings almost all day. The first one, she noted, was a networking meeting with Andy Emmel, a former co-worker. He had contacted her a couple of weeks ago, said he was looking for a job, and asked if she had time to meet as part of his job search. Of course, Margret had said yes. Her cousin had gone through a job transition a few years ago, and she knew how tough it could be. There were no available jobs for Andy at HGW at the moment, but he was a skilled chemist and loyal worker, and she felt confident that he had something to offer her group of friends and peers.

When the receptionist called to let Margret know that Andy had arrived, she grabbed a notebook and headed to the lobby. As she walked by her boss's office, he called out. He asked her to join a group conference call in one hour. It was important, her boss said.

"Sure!" she said, knowing that he rarely convened the group at the last second. She would have to be there.

In the lobby, Margret greeted Andy warmly. It was great to see him after so much time. With her unscheduled call looming, she quickly led him to a conference room to get things started.

On the way, Margret asked Andy about some mutual acquaintances and about his family. It had been a while, and he had plenty of updates.

As they sat and got settled, he continued to reminisce about some of their former colleagues, and asked if she could remember others who were outside of their pharmacy group. She could recall only some.

Over Andy's shoulder, Margret glanced at the clock. Ten minutes had already elapsed. She had started this conversation, but didn't want to step on his toes to get things back on track. But she would need time to prep for that call.

Taking advantage of a lull, she opened her notebook and asked outright:

"So, what can I do, Andy? Tell me how I can help." He was a good guy, great colleague, and her offer was genuine.

Andy cleared his throat and looked at the notebook in his lap. It was evident that his job search was taking a toll on him. His face fell, and his earlier enthusiasm nearly vanished.

"Well . . ." he started. Then he commenced to give her the background on what happened.

It was a really tough story. A long story. A tale of broken promises and betrayal among co-workers. He got the bad end of the stick once everything was said and done, and he expressed how poorly he thought he'd been treated when he was laid off. But he didn't seem to be doing much better now than when it occurred months before. Hoping to help her understand the experience, Andy even shared what Margret guessed had to be confidential details about his boss and the company. That thought concerned her. She wondered if any of her former HGW colleagues ever had these types of conversations. She didn't think it was very wise.

Another glance over Andy's shoulder showed that time was dwindling fast. Andy hadn't even mentioned what type of position he was seeking now.

"Right, let me tell you about my background," he said when asked.

Margret wasn't in time to stop him, and she cared too much about interrupting her friend to ask for an abbreviated version. But he was already giving her the full explanation of his resume. There was a lot of detail. *Too* much detail. More than anyone else had offered at one time, and it was eating into their networking opportunity.

Andy finally finished, and then he asked, "Could you tell me more about what you guys do here at HGW?"

Margret stared at him in surprise. Did he not *already* know? Had he not looked at the website?

"No, I didn't," he chuckled. "Just so busy looking for work. Figured you could tell me as we caught up."

Another glance at the clock. Now she would have to hurry this meeting if she was going to give Andy any helpful information. But then, she realized, she shouldn't be running this meeting at all.

Still, Margret gave him a high-level summary of the company's products. She explained its markets and described their target customers. And she wondered—had he been doing this with everyone? Was he expecting others to run his meetings like this? He was asking pertinent questions as she spoke, but Margret couldn't understand what they had to do with his job search.

There was an unexpected knock on the door. Her boss opened it. The group had decided to gather ahead of the call. They needed her.

Margret turned back to Andy once the door closed. She felt terrible, but she would have to cut their meeting short.

"Guess we kind of ran long, huh?" he said with a nod. Then he began to speak quickly. "Well, any help you can give . . ."

Margret waited. But nothing came. She wished that he would offer her some direction.

"I'm not sure yet what you're looking for," she said. "And unfortunately there's nothing available here right now."

Andy tapped on his still-unopened notebook.

"Do you know of any other companies with job openings? I mean, since you're working, maybe you hear of things?"

She shook her head. Knowing such things wasn't part of her day-to-day job, and she wasn't connected in pharmacy circles anymore.

There was an awkward silence, but this time she didn't know how to fill it. She had fully intended to help, but he had given her nothing to go on, and she was about to send him away with nothing.

I have some suggestions of other people he might contact, she thought. But he doesn't seem prepared enough to meet them. Besides, she wasn't sure she wanted to endorse him at this time anyway. He didn't seem to know what he was looking for.

"Well, we should at least stay in touch," Margret proposed, standing up. "I'll let you know right away if something comes up. How about a resume?"

Andy handed her a creased document from within his unopened notebook. He grinned sheepishly. He clearly understood that this meeting hadn't turned out the way either of them had intended. But in a final show of professionalism, he held out his hand.

"It was great to see you again," Andy said as she shook it. "And yes, please do keep me in mind."

He grabbed his things, and she walked him to the reception area. On the way out, she glanced at the clock once more. Fifty-nine minutes with Andy Emmel, and while they'd caught up some, they'd accomplished nothing. She felt horrible. Worse, Andy hadn't said thank you once.

⏰

Now let's take a look at a networking meeting that went a little differently.

Gene & Vicky

Gene dropped into his chair and snapped up his calendar. With the end of tax season coming, he was finally seeing the light at the end of the tunnel. At the same time, it was getting busier than ever as the April 15 deadline approached. On his to-do list today: Pluck out more of his clients' W2s from an eight-inch stack of mail and return at least a dozen calls before five. Then there was email. And daily review meetings to prep for.

His phone rang. Gene dropped the calendar and picked up the handset.

"Gene Erazo," he answered far more relaxed than he felt.

"Gene, it's Vicky. I'm at the Starbucks down the street and thought I'd bring you a coffee for our nine o'clock meeting."

Gene sat up and grabbed the calendar again. Vicky? Her name was there, but her face was missing from his mind. Had he made this appointment?

"Gene, did I lose you?"

"A latte would be fantastic; thank you for offering," he responded, still in a relaxed tone. If she was polite enough to offer, he would be polite enough to accept. But he gritted his teeth. How had this happened? How had he scheduled something in the busiest time of year?

"Latte it is," Vicky said. "See you in a few minutes."

Ten minutes later, Gene showed her into his office, closing the door behind them. Her name was ringing a bell now, but he was still wracking his brain to place her face. He felt terrible that he would have to admit this. Worse, he didn't know if he could commit to an hour for an unplanned meeting.

"Thank you again for taking the time to meet, Gene," Vicky said as she placed her folio on the table. "I know you're in your busy season, so I won't keep you long."

Gene sat across from her with a tense smile.

"Just a reminder as to our connection," Vicky continued, settling herself in. "Darcey Askins, who sends her hellos, suggested I reach out to you. It was quite a few weeks ago. She warned that you were about to hit tax season, but she insisted that we might be able to help each other network. So, thank you, again, for your time."

Darcey! thought Gene, letting out a subtle sigh of relief. It finally came back to him. Darcey was his former business partner. She mentioned Vicky at a party months ago and that she was looking for an accounting job. He knew he wouldn't have scheduled Vicky if it wasn't important. But now that he realized it was a networking meeting, he wished he could have put it off till after the 15th. He could hear emails rolling in behind him even as they sat there, and the red light on his phone was demanding his attention.

"But even though we're networking," Vicky went on as though reading his mind, "I'll only take twenty minutes of your time."

Twenty minutes. He'd heard that before. What she meant was an hour, and he didn't have that. He glanced at the clock again. Their meeting had to start *now*.

"Here is my situation," Vicky said, one step ahead. She opened her folio. "It's a fairly common story these days: I was caught up in downsizing at Sommer Company. I know you don't have job openings here for me, but I just really value the chance to make contact and discuss a thing or two."

Luka, Gene's assistant, poked his nose in the door.

"A reminder about your ten o'clock review meeting," he said, putting a stack of material on Gene's desk. "They're coming to your office."

The review meeting! That was pushed up to today and was less than an hour away. If his meeting with Vicky was like any other, he wouldn't be prepared.

Luka left the room. The door clicked closed.

"No problem with time, Gene," Vicky said, reading his mind again. "I promised—only twenty minutes."

She jumped right back in.

"I met Darcey through her daughter. Casey was getting her MBA while I was getting my Bachelor's. As you may know, she went into public accounting, where she has begun a stellar career. Once I finished my degree, and through my relationship with Casey, I joined her uncle's company, a small foundry, as staff accountant. I earned my way into more responsibility and worked closely with Boyd as he got ready to sell the business before retiring. Now that the work is complete, I am beginning to look at new opportunities."

Vicky's demeanor was steady. She didn't come off as negative or apologetic, given her circumstances. Gene admired her attitude; being out of work was not easy. He knew by experience.

"I have nearly eight years in finance and accounting," she continued. "Mostly in the foundry, a small to mid-size organization. And while I think I'd like to find a similar role, I'd like to focus my questions for you on your perceptions of some possible career directions."

Gene hesitated. He wasn't sure he was the right person to give answers on career direction.

Again, Vicky seemed to read his thoughts.

"I've been asking several people these same questions. Different perspectives on the same thing are important, and I would really value your thoughts." He glanced at the clock again. He was sure this is where things would get out of hand, but he gave her the benefit of the doubt anyway. She seemed to have a handle on what she wanted out of the meeting.

"Sure," Gene said. "Fire away."

Vicky asked Gene about growth areas that he was seeing with his clients. Were things changing? Was that influencing the industry on a broader basis? Did he foresee anything that would make the accounting world different?

The past several weeks had given Gene plenty to talk about in terms of industry trends. He shared the high points over the next ten minutes or so. As he did, Vicky busily scribbled notes in her notebook, asking pertinent questions along the way. He grinned pleasantly in spite of being stressed about time. She was actually taking him seriously, and asking questions about subjects that he could talk about.

After he finished his last thought, Vicky tapped her pen on her notebook thoughtfully.

"You've actually answered my other questions," she smiled. "Also, if you don't mind sharing—who else would you suggest I connect with as part of my networking?"

He'd been asked this before. Usually it was uncomfortable giving out names, but Vicky seemed to have her act together. She clearly knew what she was seeking and she showed her gratitude for being there. Now he understood why Darcey had insisted she reach out, and he didn't hesitate to give her a name.

"Eldon Hibert," he said. Eldon was a good referral, and Gene knew Eldon would appreciate Vicky's sharp and together approach. "He's retiring in a few years, but he seems to know everyone in financial circles in the north part of the city. Go ahead and use my name. He's an old friend and long-term client."

Vicky wrote down the information and smiled. Without taking any more time, she closed her folio and put away her pen.

"Thanks so much, Gene. Your time was very helpful. As I said at the beginning of our meeting, I want to be sensitive about your schedule." She gathered her things into a neat pile and folded her hands. "But one last question: How can I be helpful to *you*?"

Gene was taken aback. What jobseeker asks a question like this?

"Um . . . I can't think of anything at the moment . . ."

"The company that purchased Boyd's company is called Hehmans & Granville. I would be very happy to introduce you to their lead financial consultant if you think that would be beneficial. I worked closely with him during the sale. I'm sure they'd be glad to know of a terrific accounting firm."

He found himself smiling again. That was extremely thoughtful, and he'd long wanted to connect with that firm, but had no way of doing so.

"That would be wonderful. Thank you."

She smiled and stood up, extending her hand. He shook it.

"Thank you again, Gene," she said. "It was a pleasure to meet you."

He walked her to the door, and a quick glance at the clock showed that he still had over a half hour to prepare for the review meeting. She had actually stuck to twenty minutes.

"I'll be sure to tell Darcey hello for you once I let her know we had a chance to meet," Vicky said. "Have a great rest of the week."

"Thank you, Vicky. And thank you, again, for the coffee."

This Book Is for *You*

You could probably relate to some part of the previous two stories. As you saw, some networking meetings go just a little more smoothly (not to mention more effectively) than others. But it's not just chance or luck that determines whether a meeting goes well. It's skill—skill that can be learned and perfected with practice. This book will break down the successful networking meeting into its essential parts and give you the tools needed to make your own powerful meetings. Before that though, here is bit of necessary background on why the model was built.

Both authors of this book are retained executive search firm professionals. Executive search firms are hired by other companies to find new executive leaders for their organizations. As recruiting professionals, we're something like hiring managers for the company, at the executive level.

Because of the nature of the industry, recruiters, along with hiring managers are contacted literally every day to network as part of someone's job search. It's a sensible step in a executive (actually, *any*) jobseeker's strategy, but we have come to dread this oft-repeated request, regardless of how much we appreciate meeting these bright individuals.

"Hello. This is Susan SuperExec. I was referred to you because

I'm looking for a new job. I'm networking, and I want to meet with you."

Why dread these meetings when these talented professionals are our bread and butter? Because the meetings are almost always ineffective. In fact, some are *so* ineffective that it would have been better if the jobseeker had not called at all. And other meetings, while adequate enough, simply miss their full potential.

Over time, I (and my colleague/co-author) began to see what was consistently going wrong. On occasion, I also saw what was going right. I took more notes. What I ultimately observed was that the foundation of the networking meeting was being overlooked entirely. Potentially terrific networking meetings were suffering fatal blows. Those meetings were not well planned, well run, or even meaningful. They *certainly* didn't have mutuality or gratitude.

I shared these notes with my peers—people who are also frequently asked to network—and they overwhelmingly agreed that most networking meetings are entirely too long, problematic, and ineffective. Thus, *The 20-Minute Networking Meeting.*

The 20-Minute Networking Meeting is written from a hiring and recruiting perspective, and will tell you what works for the people you are contacting and hoping to impress. Step-by-step, we will analyze the structure of successful networking meetings and show you how you can put the *20MNM* model to work for yourself.

Now let's take a look at why networking is so crucial for a job-search.

Why Networking Is So Important

(Or: Hey, Friend, Your Job Market Is Hiding from You)

Perhaps you haven't given this much thought, but in spite of the plethora of online tools for jobseekers, most roles are not filled by online resume databases *or* community job boards.

Where *does* one find those jobs? Well, in the *invisible* job market, of course!

You may have heard of it before, and yes, it does exist. The invisible (or hidden) job market consists of job openings that are not advertised or publicly announced. These positions are filled by (or sometimes created for) candidates who come to an employer's attention through employee recommendations, referrals from trusted associates, recruiters, or direct contact with the candidates who may be interviewing for these jobs.

And where would this invisible job market *be*?

You're standing in it. It's all around you, all the time. It's there when you pick up your phone and when you send an email. In fact, it's the very *rumor* of job opportunities that you've heard about, well before seeing them posted somewhere. And get this— it's estimated that a whopping 70% of *all* jobs are obtained through people you know!

So how does one *become* part of the invisible job market, you ask?

Occasionally through recruiters or hiring managers like us. Or the magic portal into the Invisible Dimension. That one's hard to find, though, so networking is your best bet.

Networking, you say with a grimace. **Does it really come down to networking?**

Yes, it does. But the good news is that it's easier than you think! Networking, to the casual practitioner, is all about who you know, rather than what you know. While there's truth to that, it doesn't tell the whole story. The reality is if you haven't developed networking skills, then who you know simply won't matter. In fact, undeveloped networking skills will be the leading cause of closed doors and unanswered calls. But build those skills and you'll be adding valuable contacts and useful information that will take you anywhere you want to go. That's not conjecture. That's tried and true by some of the most admired leaders in business.

<><><><><><><><><><><><><><><><><><><><><><><><><><><><><><><><><>

TIP
The longer you maintain a healthy network,
the more powerful it becomes with each passing year.
Take advantage of it *now* and empower your future.

<><><><><><><><><><><><><><><><><><><><><><><><><><><><><><><><><>

What It is, What It Does, and Why It Works

While this book's information will give you a leg up on all kinds of networking, we're going to focus on the topic as it relates to jobseekers. The next statement sums up the importance of establishing a vibrant network:

No one is going to hire you if no one knows you exist. Right? Right.

But your chances increase tenfold if you've at least been *introduced* to a hiring authority by a friend, family member or neighbor—or perhaps even by someone you've just met.

If you know one person, and that person knows another, you have a valid and working (however small) network. Imagine if your network included dozens of people. Or hundreds. With a network this large, you could certainly achieve your goals. You would surely find out about the invisible job market. And there's no doubt you'd find out who's hiring.

But let's take a closer look at how that works.

Loosely defined, networking is the practice of meeting with other people with a specific purpose in mind. (In your case, it would be to find your first or next terrific job.) I've mentioned that this practice is imperative to job search. If you are someone returning to the workforce after time off for family, military service, or even personal reasons, networking becomes even more important.

Returning to basics, people have to know who you are. *Personally.* No amount of social networking or LinkedIn connections will ever replace *personal* relationship building. Nor is there any cover letter or well-crafted resume that's going to get the job (hunt) done better or faster. And while there are job boards, advertisements, online applications, mailed inquiries, and other such virtual job-search methods, will such opportunities be in your field or things you'd even be interested in?

Odds are slim.

But for the sake of argument, let's say you *do* find something online. Can you imagine the hundreds of other applicants you'd be competing with just to be *looked* at? It suddenly makes the idea of finding a magic portal a little more appealing, doesn't it?

Which takes us back to networking.

I mentioned earlier that 70% of all jobs are awarded only in the hidden job market. If you're aspiring to be a business leader, that figure jumps to 80% because there are even less company leadership roles available. So, if 70-80% of jobs are obtained through networking, doesn't it make sense to spend the same amount of your time focused on face-to-face activities?

Resumes and application submissions often end up in a review pile, if not a recycle pile, and that will do you no good.

So what must be done? You must get on your feet. You gotta network.

◇◇◇

All resumes must be sifted and studied. There are piles, there are those who sift through piles, and there are the weeks, and sometimes months it take to do so. Face-to-face meetings are the way to cut ahead of the competition. Efficient, to the point, with contact. *Then* will you be visible in the invisible job market.

◇◇◇

The good news is that you already have a network! Every person you know is in it. And—every person you meet expands it. Professional trade groups are a great place to get things moving. Seminars and functions geared toward networking are even better. (There's no better place than these to hone your skills before holding the meetings that count.)

But w*ait, wait,* you say. If 70-80% of my search work should be face-to-face meetings, what about the other 20-30% of my time?

Glad you asked. Online postings are a great place to "see what's out there," but still a second choice to in-person networking. If you must use the web, use your 20-30% time searching those online postings. A better idea, however, would be to use that time to correspond via email and follow up with brief thank-yous for those completed face-to-face meetings.

<><><><><><><><><><><><><><><><><><><><><><><><><><><><><><><><><><><>

POTENTIAL NETWORKING CONTACTS:

- Former co-workers, peers, and staff from your previous employer
- Professionals you've met at trade associations, conferences, or training programs
- Vendors, suppliers, and clients you've worked with
- Consultants you've worked with
- Friends, neighbors, and members of your faith community
- Fellow alumni from the high school, college(s) or trade school(s) you attended
- Fraternities and Sororities
- Career guidance counselors from your current/former college or university. (Note: Often there are *alumni* services, too, so you don't need to be a student to take advantage of the help!)
- Fellow members of academic, civic and athletic clubs (Former athlete? Teammates and coaches are a great place to start!)
- Professional service providers, such as your accountant, attorney, and tax preparer
- Government, County, or City Workforce Centers

<><><><><><><><><><><><><><><><><><><><><><><><><><><><><><><><><><><>

Also, don't forget that there are many networking groups designed specifically for your background and profession. Take a moment to find such groups through LinkedIn or even your alma mater's Career Services or Alumni Relations office or website. Barring those options, and as mentioned above, many city and/or counties maintain Workforce Centers. They are designed to help jobseekers find employment for themselves. Just hop on the web for a look!

How Networking (*Really*) Works

As mentioned a few times already, most jobs are filled by contacts that come from personal relationships. Whether intentional or not, it's the common approach in business. For instance, a strong recommendation from a trusted source (i.e. friend; family member; former co-worker) could be all that's needed for you to get an interview with a hiring manager. Decision-makers look to *their* networks for valued suggestions and referrals, too. And as there's no way someone can *know* a candidate by reading a piece of paper outlining a work history [resume], their contacts' trusted word is paramount. For example, when the search for an employee starts, the first question a hiring decision-maker usually asks is:

"Hey—who do you know that can do this job?"

The answer, more often than not, is:

"Let me think about whom I know."

And *justlikethat*, the networking has begun. Don't you want to be the person who comes to mind right away?

Here's a scenario. Let's presume there are two potential candidates with similar backgrounds. We'll call them Passive Candidate and Active Candidate. Both have experience, both are in the same profession, and both or networking for similar jobs in the same city. Essentially, they're in the exact same scenario.

Passive Candidate has been slow to start the networking process, focusing instead on combing the Internet and studying online postings and want ads. He's comfortable taking it easy, and using this methodology, he's set up a few networking meetings.

Active Candidate has put her time toward active networking. By phoning some former co-workers, sending out emails to contacts at other organizations, and scheduling lunches with several employed friends, Active Candidate succeeds in conducting twenty-five networking meetings. (Remember—*anyone* you know is in your network. And as one *never* knows who holds key information to your job search, your contact base can easily add up to twenty-five or more people.) Now Active Candidate and Passive Candidate are quickly on two different paths.

Just to make things interesting, though, let's say that Active Candidate didn't feel too hot about the result of some of her meetings. It hampers some of her efforts, and consequently her confidence. We'll come back to this again in a second.

Okay, to recap what we have so far: two people, same set of circumstances, two different approaches, and a number of networking meetings. Now let's develop the invisible job market to see how they do.

Switch to the perspective of the hiring manager who is looking to fill a new role. He has talked to those around him about the position—"Hey, who do you know that can do this job?"—and word has begun to spread through his trusted group (network) of peers, former colleagues, and friends (whether around town or around the country). As it does, those people share this information with *their* network of peers, former colleagues, and friends, letting them know that a new job is up for grabs at ABC Company.

Voilà! A posting on the invisible job market exists.

With all the pieces on the table, it should be clear that Active Candidate has much more of an edge. But let's look more closely at how.

If *any* of those twenty-five people whom Active Candidate happened to meet with is in the extended network of the hiring manager, Active Candidate's going to hear word of the opportunity. Plain and simple. To be more specific, people talk, and people pass forward this kind of information. With each new person who learns of this new job, it can be surmised that the information will be disseminated to at least one, if not a few more people, until there is a widely cast net. Active Candidate is going to hear of the opportunity, *just by being in the network.*

By contrast, Passive Candidate likely doesn't even know the job exists yet. Why? Because it's not posted, and because it's less likely that Passive Candidate's smaller network overlaps with the hiring manager's extended network. (Yes, it's *possible*—just less likely.) So, without actively growing his network, Passive Candidate is going to miss an opportunity because he put more time into postings than people.

This should make it crystal clear how Active Candidate stands a pretty good chance of getting a face-to-face meeting with ABC Company. Agreed?

Now let's address Active Candidate's not-so-good meeting that we mentioned earlier, just so we can draw another networking point.

Let's say, for sake of our networking argument, that word from the hiring manager has finally made its way through the grapevine to one of the people that Active Candidate met with.

But for some reason that meeting didn't go well. Maybe it was bumpy, maybe someone was tired, or maybe the contact was somewhat reluctant to meet in the first place. (Sometimes we have bad days.) Even if this were the case, Active Candidate has become an extension of the total network anyway. She immediately becomes the first qualified person to pop into her contact's head, bumpy meeting or not. That alone makes her *far* more likely to get the job than Passive Candidate, who is still at home basking in the glow of his computer screen. Wouldn't you say?

And *justlikethat*, Active Candidate has become visible in the invisible job market. Passive Candidate, on the other hand, simply wouldn't know any better.

Becoming the Best (Networker) You Can Be

Earlier, I stated that most of the networking meetings I partici-pate in are ineffective. These are executives, mind you; people who have had many years in the workforce to master them. The reason for the ineffectiveness is because many people in job tran-sition focus much of their attention on LinkedIn profiles and resumes—how to write them, how to format them, how to make sure that keywords are highlighted, and how often to send or share them. By contrast, they don't think much about their face-to-face meetings—the *one* thing that gets jobs. And yet, from a recruitment perspective, networking is where the major problems are.

The fact is, you can tweak your resume from here to kingdom come and it will not make much difference. After all, how per-fectly written does a resume need to be before you get a call? How many do you need to send out to get even one response? How many LinkedIn connections must you have to get an appointment?

But—what if you were to become an expert *networker*? Some-one who is well informed and well regarded by a large group of connections? Someone for whom each interaction is a job-seeking home run? Someone who has a built a network that is actively engaged in helping *you* find your first or next great job? Now we're talking!

Here are the three things you want to get out of a networking meeting:

- Gather some new information
- Add new contacts to your list
- Gain an evangelist (Say what? Don't worry, I'll explain.)

Just what kind of new information are we talking about? A clearer understanding of what your job market is looking for, and where you fit in that market, are a couple of examples.

For instance, does the legal profession still need lawyers and legal aides, or is it dying off? Where does the demand now stand for your nursing degree? Does technology affect the way you do your work, and do you have enough training to keep up with its evolution?

Get a handle on such information and you may be surprised how it impacts your job search, not to mention how it will inform your career choices.

Before we get into depth, let's clear our networking path by debunking some networking myths.

Networking Myths

(Or: Never Ever Believe These Things)

Networking gets a pretty bad rap. This is often due to misperception and misunderstanding. Let's debunk some myths about networking and deconstruct some common mistakes. Here are some ways of thinking that you want to leave behind:

- I'm just wasting my time
- Networking is just schmoozing
- The longer the meeting, the better
- No one wants to meet with an inexperienced worker
- It's helpful for *others* to have the chance to meet with *me*
- A networking meeting is when I give a detailed description of my background.
- Off the cuff is best; I'll figure out each meeting when I get there
- My networking contacts will find me a job!

Now let's debunk them.

"I'm Just Wasting My Time."

Pssst—remember the previous section? The part about how 70-80% of jobs are found through networking? Believe me, it's no waste of time.

Meeting with people (both new and old contacts) is probably the most important thing you can do while looking for work. Your networking meetings could surely lead to job connections, but the networking meetings might lead to *other* opportunities that you hadn't yet thought about.

For instance, your meetings could get you caught up on happenings in your current or future industry. Being knowledgeable and informed is an important impression to leave during your meetings. Or you might learn of *other* business opportunities such as contract work or temporary work, or even *new professions* related to your background that you never knew existed. That alone is a *life-changer*! And feedback? Absolutely. This in turn will sharpen your networking skill set, which in turn will improve your chances of obtaining your networking goals—including getting a job.

But these are just a *few* benefits of networking. So get rid of this mentality. Networking is never a waste of time.

— MYTH —

"Networking Is Just Schmoozing."

Mark this with a pen. Lots of people commit the sin of schmoozing. Shooting the breeze is enjoyable, but not if you're the person who has work piling up back at the office. Save the irrelevant chitchat. If you don't, you'll come across more as a social-minded networker than a professional tracking down an employment opportunity. Worse, if you have "the gift of gab," you might run the risk of coming across as "salesy." Believe me: I see this often. And also believe me when I say it's irritating. Instead, present yourself and speak like the competent professional you are.

— MYTH —

"The Longer The Meeting, The Better."

I always grin when I hear this one. Why? Because long meetings are what keep people from networking in the first place.

A networking meeting is a chance to make a positive connection. An hour-long litany about your background, accomplishments, family pedigree and/or qualifications is not positive and you will be seen as someone who "doesn't get it." That's not good. You can't forget that the people you're meeting with have busy lives, too. Taking an excessive amount of his or her time appears inconsiderate. It also reveals that you don't know how to run a crisp, mutually beneficial networking meeting (which harks back to my observation that so many networking meetings are ineffective because they're not well-planned or well-run). That's a lot of counts against you. Keep things brief.

— MYTH —

"No One Wants to Meet With an Inexperienced Worker."

Au contraire! In fact, many professionals *will* meet with inexperienced workers. While it's understandable to believe that busy contacts have little time to meet with new or inexperienced job-seekers, running a clean, polished meeting is what makes the difference. Keeping it at 20 minutes is perfect, and is something most busy professionals can handle.

Additionally, those same people know what it's like to enter a job market, too. Some even know what it's like to enter it a *second* or *third* time (say, due to layoffs). Most will respect your proactive approach (not to mention that you've kept the meeting brief and structured). After all, a well-prepped, well put-together professional is what *any* job market is looking for.

— MYTH —

"It's Helpful for *Others* to Have the Chance to Meet with *Me*."

Please—never expect that others will you see you as someone they need to impress. I see this mistake often. Remember that you're waiting for your next opportunity, and that an attitude of entitlement or expectation will backfire on you in grand fashion. While you may have had pull and influence in the past, it is important to remember that at this moment what you have to give in return is less than what you stand to earn. Which is fine. It's part of job transition. But consideration is key here.

— MYTH —

"A Networking Meeting Is When I Give a Detailed Description of My Background."

This myth overlaps with "The Longer the Meeting, the Better."

But they are different. While an overview of your education, qualifications and/or experience is an essential part of your networking meetings, too much information is not welcome. Not if it isn't asked for. You're there to *learn* as much as you're there to network.

This point is important. You see, your networking contacts are probably not hiring managers. While you will eventually meet those people, your other contacts will think about jobs in fairly general buckets. Lawyer. Derrickman. Nurse. Mechanic. Store Manager. Lab Tech. Personal Trainer. They need to know just enough about your background to connect you with an opportunity if one pops into mind when they are reminded of something relevant. More than that makes things confusing and less memorable. Why? It's simply too difficult to keep track of so much information, especially if the purpose of the meeting is general networking.

Listening is learning, and networking is give-and-take.
Don't be tempted to talk all about yourself
or what you're in need of.

— MYTH —

"Off the Cuff Is Best; I'll Figure Out Each Meeting When I Get There."

What jobseeker would go into any meeting unprepared? Especially a meeting that could ultimately lead you to a job? Remember, this is *employment* we're talking about. If employment is an important factor in your life at all, you can understand the importance of prep here. Besides, weren't you always able to tell when someone came to work unready or underprepared?

From a recruiting and hiring standpoint, it is *immediately* apparent when someone has not prepared for a networking meeting. A CEO in transition came in for such a meeting with me once, plopped down in the chair, and took off talking in all directions—how talented her peers felt she was, how skilled she was at change management, how strategic her vision was for her industry. I sat across from her and wondered how any of it was relevant to *me*, her networking contact. Now, don't get me wrong—I appreciate spontaneity as much as the next person, but start with something structured. An agenda or quick overview of what you'd like to discuss, for instance, would be fabulous. It's simply nice to know what we will be talking about.

◇◇

An unprepared agenda will have undesired consequences. *Always* be prepared for your meetings.

◇◇

— MYTH —

"My Networking Contacts Will Find Me a Job!"

Most of your contacts are fulfilling their own job responsibilities. More often than not, those responsibilities are not recruiting/hiring responsibilities. Accept the fact that virtually none of your networking meetings will immediately lead to a current opportunity, and remind yourself that this isn't the point to networking anyway. It's about *ultimate*, not immediate, gratification. You simply want to get the "lay of the land." Bringing yourself up to date on what's happening in your industry is a good goal, for example, as is finding out who's out there, and who might be looking for you.

Think of it this way: If a friend of a friend called you right now to request a networking meeting, would you know of an immediate job opening for that person? Would you be prepared to help a banker? A college professor? A machine operator in the packaging industry? Not likely. But when you *do* hear of an opening, you'll probably remember the new friend who requested a 20-minute networking meeting with you, right? Of course you will. And that person will remember you, too.

On recruiters and hiring managers: The same applies when you connect with us. The likelihood that any recruiter will have an open assignment that fits your background is very, very small. Job-fulfillment is nearly always dictated by the needs of the company or our clients. We often don't even know what job we'll be filling next. So how could we plug you into something we don't even know exists at the moment?

◇◇◇

Your contacts are not recruiters or hiring managers.
Never expect a single networking meeting to lead to a
job. Patience is the name of the game.

◇◇◇

Now that we've debunked some of the myths that surround networking, we'll focus on the hurdle that keeps jobseekers from taking that first step. Let's start with a Real-World Perspective.

Real-World Perspective

("So You Want Me to Go Out There and Grovel, Huh?")

I got a call from a company leader who happened to know my cousin. This very experienced individual, a senior vice president of supply chain, has an extensive background and pretty impressive accreditation. His job search, however, was at a standstill.

"How's the networking going?" I asked.

"It's nearly impossible getting responses from online applications," he expressed in frustration.

I let him know that online postings were rarely effective for job-search (for the reasons you now know) and reassured him that he had a right to feel this way. Then I asked my question again.

"How is the networking going?"

Happy to have another opportunity to vent, he expressed the difficulties of getting through to recruiters and hiring managers, too. I smiled at this—it is a common gripe—and took the opportunity to explain that by nature of the industry we aren't outplacement counselors (who give job-search guidance), nor do we exist to find jobs for jobseekers. Rather, we do work for our *clients*, much like any other business would; it just happens that our commodity of trade is executives instead of, say, products or goods. I had to ask again.

"So, how is the *networking* going?"

It was as though he already knew the truth. He sighed and bottom-lined his answer.

"So you want me to go out there and grovel, huh?"

If I could only tell you how often I have heard this. Not just the tone of voice, but the mentality. No, it is not easy to ask for help. But it's not groveling, either.

No one is going to put opportunity in your lap, no matter who you are, and there are no shortcuts. You must take control of your own circumstances by learning to call on the advice and knowledge of others. To do so is to control the direction of your job search, if not your career.

Now let's take a closer look at why this jobseeker felt so discouraged by the thought of getting out there and networking.

What Makes Networking So Difficult?

(Or: Okay, Okay, I'll Do It. But It's So Hard!)

Yes, networking is hard work. But you're not alone. Most people are hesitant to network, and when the purpose is to find a new job, they're even more reluctant. And I'm referring to experienced professionals here, who hold one-on-one meetings *every day!*

Let's discuss this.

Maybe you don't like the idea of networking because you feel like you're intruding. Maybe you feel like your request for time is an unwelcome detour into someone's day. Or maybe you just don't feel like people want to sit with a stranger.

Very understandable. Really. Because your feelings are probably right. (I told you I was going to give you the perspective from the other side of the desk!) And there's a reason—a reason that was addressed at the very beginning of this book: too many networking meetings are too long and too unfocused. And long meetings simply don't honor the busy schedule of the other person.

Remember that every person who agrees to a networking meeting is giving you a *gift* of time. Think of it this way. If your contact happens to work fifty hours per week, your meeting just made it a fifty-one-hour week. That extra hour is because of your meeting! That translates to less friend time, less family time, less time for other pursuits, or even for sleep!

Here's one more way to look at it. If your contact is a consultant that charges $200 per hour—say like a lawyer or another kind of service professional, a one-hour networking meeting with you just cost them $200 in billable hours (or at the very least, an hour of selling time). How often do *you* give a gift worth $200?

Probably not too often.

◇◇

The time someone gives you is a gift. What does an hour mean to *you*? Is it worth $200 in billable hours? How often do *you* give a $200 gift?

◇◇

Ultimately, such long, inconsiderate meetings are what give networking a bad name and why people avoid it. To compound this fear of networking, many are intimidated by the concept of it, too. People tend to envision an hour-long meeting, during which they need to be:

1. socially adept;
2. professionally impeccable; and
3. capable of the above without the need of an agenda.

If that were the case, you'd have to be a corporate and social genius armed with wit and improv skills, right? Well, no wonder you would be hesitant to network. Good thing that's not what we're talking about here.

Making Excuses

So what *am* I talking about? I'm talking about making contact, conducting brief meetings, and following up. *That's it*. It's something that, in many ways, you've likely been doing for a while. Of course, the circumstances of networking are a bit different, but you can't let that get in your way. Yes, it's tough not to feel embarrassed or unsure about doing it, but it should *never* be a reason to avoid networking.

Over the years, I've witnessed professionals—including company leaders—busy themselves with all sorts of "job-seeking activities" to avoid networking for a job, all because of the feeling of embarrassment, shyness, or apprehension. You probably know these kinds of excuses, too—like tweaking and re-tweaking your resume, perpetually checking emails or online job posts, or even constant "prep" for a (hopeful) job interview. It's hard to imagine, but I've even known executives who have shopped for the right outfit or shoes that are "a must" before getting an interview! I assure you—I've heard them all.

So, what do you *do* to get rid of these fears and embarrassments? Commit yourself to learning how to conduct a structured networking meeting and remind yourself that no matter how well or poorly a meeting may go, you're already doing *much* more for your job search than before—even more than some of the most experienced professionals out there.

Three Real Perspectives on Networking

The idea of networking hits all of us differently. The following examples highlight three different networking perspectives. I chose composite examples based on what I hear all the time. Here's what a few had to say, followed by my reactions.

Gerardo

Gerardo's position as sales engineer for a national auto parts chain was recently eliminated. Having worked for a competing chain, he feels he's burned all bridges and that he's run out of networking contacts as a result.

"Besides already knowing everybody there is to know in my region, I also pull 60-hour weeks, partly in the factory, partly on the road. But because of that, combined with time needed for family, there's been no chance to make professional connections. Now that I need to start networking, I feel like there's no one to connect *with*. I'm not a talker either and am not great with words. How am I going to keep these conversations going? I don't want to make a fool of myself."

Great question. But first, don't worry about having a limited network. Many people find themselves starting from the beginning. Even if you're not a talker, you'll do fine with the model of The 20-Minute Networking Meeting. *It's designed to help you construct and carry a conversation.*

Sometimes professionals feel that, despite their accomplishments inside their organizations, they have not taken the time to build networks outside their organizations. If you have family members or friends outside your professional circle, they are a start. So is your neighborhood. So is your faith community or civic group. Former staff and colleagues are great contacts. You probably have a broader network than you realize if you just consider who you already know.

Ashley

Ashley has a degree in Computer and Information Technology. She wants to find a position that allows her to build computer-networking infrastructures. But it's slow going. While her people skills are satisfactory, she's shy. And due to Ashley's affinity for technology, her primary job-searching method is web-surfing.

"I'm faster on a computer," Ashley says. "I know how to use all the job boards and databases better than most people, which gives me an edge. And it gives me a farther reach than what's near me. I am hoping that I can find a job over the net without help from anybody."

You can't really conduct an effective job search in a vacuum. People *hire people—not your technology—and making personal connections is going to be key to finding your perfect job. Don't spend*

all your time on the web. While the Internet might give you a lon-
ger geographic reach, many hiring managers will not spend time
recruiting professionals who don't already live in their market
anyway. Also try to remember that nearly everyone has a way to
access the net these days. Whether you're faster on a computer or
not, it means significantly more competition. In the end, it will be
networking *that tells you what you need to know about your spe-*
cific job market. And it will be direct contact *that puts you in front*
of decision-makers.

MY SUGGESTION:

**Try to limit online postings to only 20-30% of your available job-
search time. Use the rest of your availability to pick up the phone,
send emails, or have lunch with those who can help you make
your next connection.**

Jill

Jill, a vice president of sales, was recently fired after a disagree-
ment with her boss, the company's owner. She isn't at liberty to
say exactly what happened, but her boss is known to be difficult
to work with. Whatever the situation, Jill is actively seeking a new
position in a tough market, and is getting discouraged.

"My job-search coach wants me to start networking with
people I used to associate with through my industry sales leadership group. The truth is, I don't really know those people very
well. It's not that I mind talking to people. After all, that's what
I do for a living. But, to call people I barely know and ask for
time in the middle of their workday is going to be tough. I know
how many hours a week these people work. And they travel a
lot. How many of them are going to want to take time to meet
with me? That's the part that gives me some hesitation to start
my networking.

WHAT I SAID:

You're right about several things. Yes, you'll be contacting people you don't know well, and no, not all of them will have time to meet with you. But that's part of the nature of networking. I'm afraid that you'll just have to forge ahead with the caveats you've expressed. Start with the people you know best. Perhaps there are clients who you have "gone the extra mile for" over the years. Maybe you've assisted or trained some of your peers, or you could ask staff members you've mentored. Begin networking with people you are comfortable with and who will likely be receptive to your call.

MY SUGGESTION:

The model of *The 20-Minute Networking Meeting* recommends that you include how you can help others versus how others can help you. This is a difference-maker, and will help you feel like you're a partner and not a burden to the people you contact.
When you're ready, spend extra time on Key Question 5, about giving back to the people you meet with. (This can be found in the Great Discussion chapter.) Don't lose that sense of gratitude! It goes a long way with someone who puts a busy schedule on hold to meet with you.

OVERALL

Try to remember that networking is not about being slick and smooth. It's about developing relationships through brief, meaningful interactions over the course of time. As relationship-building *takes* time, doing this now helps you avoid networking problems down the road.

Now for the Good Stuff

So far, we've learned what networking is and why it works, and we've talked about a number of myths that surround networking for jobseekers. We've also seen some examples of professionals struggling with the idea of incorporating networking into their job searches. I hope you'll take a moment to think about your own experience, and try to identify ways some of these misperceptions have affected your search so far. But come back soon, because we're about to take a crash course in conducting the best networking meetings possible.

Now's the time for a quick coffee break.

Ready?
Let's do it!

PART II

The 20-Minute Networking Meeting

Objectives & Strategy

You made it! We'll keep this short and get right to the nitty-gritty. (Pssst—if you haven't read the first part of this book, don't cheat. Shortcuts, a professional does not take. Besides, Part II will make more sense with the context provided by Part I.)

YOUR OBJECTIVE IN JOB NETWORKING

Okay, so you're looking for work. Your top-level objective is to land a new, terrific job, right? Sure. But what if your new networking contacts don't know of open positions in the first place? Then these are your objectives in networking:

- Gather new information
- Add new contacts to your list
- Gain an evangelist

Now let's take a closer look at each of these objectives and how they will help you achieve your *20MNM* goals.

Gather New Information

WHAT IT MEANS: Listening. Questioning. Absorbing (and *writing down*) what is said to you.

THE REASON: Networking is a way to learn from contacts firsthand. It's also a chance to share what you know with your contacts to get reactions and redirection. It's quite an opportunity. You'll be giving as much as you're receiving!

You always want a *modest* goal for gathering information from any one networking meeting. Every person will have a few nuggets of value for you. Examples would be:

- Information that informs you on changes in your future functional area
- Information that helps you deduce who might be looking for help
- Information that keeps you abreast of your chosen industry or industries

VERY IMPORTANT:
Don't expect more than a few nuggets from each contact!
Remember, this is a brief *meeting*, not a seminar.

Add New Contacts to Your List

WHAT IT MEANS: Getting additional names. These could be:

- Other people in your and your contacts' industries or function
- People in your target companies or industries
- Anyone else who could help in your job search

THE REASON: Contacts—especially the way we're defining the term here—are people who know you. As it pertains to job search, they are specifically people who are connected somehow to your line of work, industry, etc. The more people who know you, the more information there is *about* you in the marketplace. The more your name is circulating in that marketplace, the more likely you will be connected to a great new opportunity.

WHY YOU WOULD DO IT: You'll be left in the dark if you don't. Do you recall that 70-80% of all jobs are obtained through people you know? And do you recall our scenario where Passive Candidate ended up in the glow of his computer while Active Candidate inserted herself into the radar of the working world? You want to avoid being like Passive Candidate.

VERY IMPORTANT:

While there are exceptions, most jobseekers land their next job not from their own original list of networking contacts, or even from the contacts gained from that original group, but through the "third ring" of people (i.e., friends of friends of friends). It's only through active networking that you'll get to the third ring. And, having worked with thousands of executives in transition, I, along with countless other hiring managers and recruiters, can attest that this is true.

◇◇◇

Many years ago, I was looking for a new job. I was referred to a business consultant, and we set up a networking meeting. Since it was a fairly distant connection, I was anticipating a cordial but not extensive session. Imagine my surprise when she pulled out a large three-ring binder full of tattered pages containing all of her business connections. She proceeded to go through the binder name by name, page by page, offering many of them to me as potential networking contacts. She must have given me twenty-five or more names! Top executives! One that I remember was a prominent CEO in a field related to my work. He took my networking meeting on her referral, and we had a fine discussion. That meeting gave me the confidence to network with other high-level professionals. Some of the contacts I made from those tattered pages turned into professional colleagues who later became clients. More than fifteen years later, I still remember the unexpected assistance from an unexpected source.

The lesson: You never know!

Gain an Evangelist

WHAT IT MEANS: A jobseeker needs an evangelist, which is someone willing to take positive action on their behalf. More than an advocate, an evangelist is like your own personal ambassador. These people will have a *major impact* on your networking. Developing one is something you must try to do with each new networking meeting by way of excellent prep and presentation.

THE REASON: Once you've got an evangelist on your side, you're on your way to twice the pay-off, but half the work. Here's what an evangelist might do for you:

- Forward your resume
- Recommend you to someone who is hiring
- Check his or her company's internal postings to see if anything is a fit for you
- Contact you later with additional ideas
- Introduce you to someone else
- Suggest you for a project

WHY YOU WOULD DO IT: Why *wouldn't* you do it? Having someone who sings your praises, recommends you to personal contacts, and thinks of you first in a job search? Hmm. Not a lot to expand on here.

Now, despite what you may think, developing this kind of contact is very, very simple. People like to help people. For most of us, it's in our nature (though the desire wanes if our time is wasted). And most people in a position to help likely got there because someone helped them first. So really, in a sense, they're not just giving, but giving back.

HOW YOU WOULD DO IT: Think about meeting new professional contacts. As you meet with those people, you will be there to learn and observe two things:

1. Their skills and abilities as related to what they do for a living.
2. How they act in a professional setting (we'll expand on that more in a second).

Now let's turn the focus to you. You'll be giving the same clear impression of how *you* act in a professional setting, and you'll also leave an impression of what *you* have to offer the working world.

When these things line up and that new contact becomes convinced by your background and experience (not by selling or persuading) that you fit within their network somewhere, that person may become an evangelist.

Make sense? Let's put it in simpler terms, just for clarity's sake: When people really like you and have an appreciation for your work history and experience (even if it's limited), they will likely want to go to bat for you. Especially if they sincerely believe your talent and offering should have a place somewhere in the working universe. Why would they do that? Well, aside from wanting to help another person, it's because having you in *their* network benefits them, too. In the long run, when you're eventually in a position to give back in the way of business, it's a relationship that already has a foundation and a history.

It is critical to keep in mind, however, that most of the time the people you are networking with are not interviewing you for a job. They will not be in a position to evaluate your skill set (they're not hiring managers), nor will they evaluate your abilities and background against a particular hiring situation (because they're not interviewing you).

On the other hand, it is important that you don't treat a networking meeting as just a social interaction or a chance to make a new friend. Those things are fine, but your main objective in networking is to make a solid, positive impression about how you act in a professional setting.

Assuming that you are meeting a networking contact for the first time, or reconnecting with someone you don't know well, you want to leave an impression that will prompt that person to recommend or refer you to others. Think about the professionals you most admire. (Past colleagues; current co-workers; leaders in your industry and so on.) What are the characteristics that you admire about them? Now think about your own positive professional characteristics. Do a few come to mind? Now is the time to show them. Here's what you want to come across in each networking meeting:

- You are positive (*upbeat tone, language, overall positivity*)
- You are strategic (*you know why you are there*)
- You are well organized (*by managing your meeting well, keeping a close tab on topics and time*)
- You are gracious (*appreciative and grateful for the time that was spent with you*)
- You follow through after a meeting (*prompt follow-up,*

meaningful ongoing interactions)

Does this sound like someone you would recommend for a job or refer to a colleague? It does to me! You've heard the phrase "It's not *what* you know, it's *who* you know." While that is certainly true in networking, there is a related sentiment that is equally true. "There's no second chance at a first impression." Leave 'em impressed!

Who You Are
(Or: Who You're *Supposed* to Be)

We've discussed your contacts and even touched on the angelic offerings of a potential evangelist. Before we get too far, however, have you thought about what type of professional *you* aspire to be? Are you someone who is well organized? Sharp? Do you manage projects and time effectively? Do you set and achieve objectives? Do others like being around you? Are you gracious to others? Do you redirect and follow up again if need be?

The demands are certainly a tall order to fill, but if you've witnessed the achievements of a successful career, then you understand that these are common characteristics. And now is the time to exhibit them yourself. Why? Because in a networking meeting, you want to showcase your professional attitude as much as—if not more than—you want to carefully explain your skills and abilities. It's a big part of that overall impression. After all, would you hire someone with great skills and poor interpersonal style? No, probably not. So would you expect your networking contacts to endorse you if you displayed poor professional-style characteristics? No, probably not.

CHARACTERISTICS YOU WANT TO EXHIBIT DURING YOUR NETWORKING MEETINGS:

Positivity

Strategic abilities

Impressive planning and organization skills

Strong communication skills

Generosity and gratitude

Follow-through

Since we're on the topic of professional integrity, here's a great example of reputation and the power of evangelism. I call it:

"Everybody Loves This Guy!"

A few years back, I conducted an executive search for a company seeking a vice president of marketing in the consumer pack-aged-goods industry. I made over 150 calls to potential candidates and sources. The first person I called recommended a friend in transition who might be a fit. His name was Mark Stone. I already had Mark Stone in my database as someone to call, but I noted the recommendation anyway. It's important to keep track of these things.

Imagine my surprise when the tenth person I called also suggested Mark Stone. Then person number thirty-one. Then person number fifty-five.

In the end, eight people suggested that I call Mark Stone about this job. Eight.

Eventually, Mark Stone and I talked about the opportunity I was recruiting for. We discussed his background, interests, and credentials. Ultimately, the search I was conducting was not a fit, but with such an army of evangelists behind him, it's hard to avoid thinking of Mark when other marketing opportunities come up. While some time has passed, his name is *still* mentioned every time a related job opens up, whether he's a fit or not, due to his professional integrity and especially due to his legions of evangelists. They're doing work for him, and quite often, Mark doesn't even know it.

I'm happy to report that Mark landed in a great new position. My guess is that he'll never be without a marketing opportunity in his career again. He's the kind of evangelist-making professional *every* jobseeker should aspire to be.

The 20-Minute Networking Meeting

What It Is and Where It Came From

Since the publication of the Executive Edition a few years back, it has come to our attention that the *20MNM* generates controversy because it calls for so little time. The question most asked is: "Can one really cover enough ground in 20 minutes?" The answer is a resounding *Yes*, and we'll show you exactly how. For the moment, allow me to explain how the material was culled from the experiences of others and actuated by a presentation I attended.

Invited to a business event that featured a local speaker and a topic I was interested in, I showed up prepared to pass the time. (Perhaps you've done such a thing before: Take articles to read, documents that need prep, and a cell phone full of emails to check). I assumed (just as everyone else did) that this was going to be a long talk, and I'd have time to catch up on other work. But I was in for a real surprise.

Just as the speaker seemed to get rolling, he finished. I remember wondering if I was late to his presentation. But everyone else seemed as surprised as I was (by the way we were all looking at one another), and the group eventually got out of their seats. We were actually *done!*

And that's when it hit me. The speaker's brevity wasn't just a welcome change to his presentation-going audience, but actually a slick strategy that brought sharp focus to his topic and made *effective use* of everyone's time. It was almost laughable in its effect. *People stuck around.* With extra time and the author's book on our hands, we were now free to be a self-engaged audience to come or go as we pleased. Many began asking meaningful questions about his material. And why wouldn't we? That was the whole reason we were there in the first place!

In retrospect, the speaker's outcome was even better than what I observed at the time. So much so that I'm now relating the story of his book and presentation to *you.*

Now *that's* impact.

After leaving the event, I took some time to understand exactly what the speaker did to pull off such a feat. Here's what happened in all its simplistic glory. Somewhere after introducing his book (which he gave to all the attendees), the author threw out some juicy bits about its contents, pulled us in *juuust* enough to capture our interest, and then cut us free. From there, with no pressure to stay or involve ourselves, the audience actually engaged, and *that was that.* It couldn't have been more perfect. Or short!

Often we attend professional presentations, workshops or classes to help our careers, and we just *know* they're going to be long, too detailed, or too irrelevant. Sometimes we want to go, and sometimes we *have* to.

Well, networking meetings can be the same in many ways. Occasionally people *want* to do them, and sometimes, they feel that they *have* to. Many times, like a presentation, the meeting becomes too long, and if it's ill-planned or lacking in focus, it holds the *contact* captive, a waste of his or her time.

I contemplated this while considering the hundreds of networking meetings I had banked in the last few years and asked myself, "What *is* too long? What is too short? Is there a happy medium?"

As I slowly pulled this information together, I also *really* began to pay attention to the clock during meetings. I observed, more often than not, that people were pushing hour-long networking meetings—whether they had requested that much time or not. And once I came to *that* realization, I decided there had to be a better way.

My conclusion, as you know by now, was that an hour is *a lot* for what actually needs to be discussed in a networking meeting. I began observing what an hour of networking time was taking away from me (work, which backed up; family time, which you can never get back; social time with friends; and, for goodness' sake, *sleep*). It was all adding up to a lot of *life*. Heck, there are barely enough hours in the day for *work!*

So next, I began to distill. I gathered the best approaches that the best networkers brought to the table and kept close track of the weakest methodologies. And of course, I did this while keeping track of time. This is what I found:

A full hour (even for an executive recruiter who is accustomed to this) *lost my attention*. Right around the thirty-minute mark, I started to consider what else I had to accomplish that day. Distraction set in as I began to stress about the work piling up behind me.

Thirty minutes was better than an hour and, yes, I was less distracted, but it's still the length of a full TV sitcom (with commercials!). And the mutual benefit was still too small. Where was the vital information about the networker? And why hadn't we hit those points in thirty full minutes?

Fifteen minutes was much better. Remembering the aforementioned speaker's short presentation, I focused on what my shorter meetings looked like. These weren't traditional networking meetings, but rather networkers dropping by or asking to just stop in and shake hands in the lobby. Fifteen minutes wasn't enough to learn about the people I was speaking with, and some of those precious minutes were being taken up by required hellos and proper goodbyes. And then I found the "happy medium."

Twenty minutes, as it turns out, is exactly the right amount of time to warm into a conversation, get a good sense of someone's background and goals, and see the person off properly. Over the course of time, this seemed to prove itself true time and time again.

Not wanting it to be just my opinion, I shared the idea with my business partners and a few other networkers. Universally, they concluded that this observation was spot-on. When the meetings were shorter they were better! Bingo!

After bringing the finer points of networking together (mind you, this is *years'* worth of networking) and collecting the experiences of a number of colleagues, a perfect, twenty-minute package of give-and-take networking emerged. Ultimately, it structured itself into *The 20-Minute Networking Meeting*. Which brings us to the book you're holding now.

The 20-Minute Networking Meeting is the distillation of decades of concepts. With the express goal of making each networking meeting do the most it can for you, it is specifically built for your job search and designed to meet the needs of both networkers and their networking contacts.

Back to it. Here are the golden rules to remember:

- Each part is **important** and has a **purpose**
- There are **five steps** and **five questions**
- You should **follow them** *exactly* so that you get a com-

mand of the process

NOTE: As you become familiar with the *20MNM* format, you *can* allow yourself flexibility by tweaking your timing and agenda. Networking is a people activity. Conversations take turns and jump off topic. This is okay, so long as you use professional discretion to get back on track when you're too far off agenda. Again, you won't always have to stick to 20 minutes. But 'til then, follow the steps 'til you know it well!

What To Do First

Before you hit the job market and start networking, you've got to be ready. Really ready. Do not begin networking (and certainly do not begin interviewing for jobs) until you're prepared.

How?

There are a lot of ways to be prepared to hit the job market—having an updated resume and a prepared "elevator speech" (explaining yourself in a relatively short amount of time); planning your networking activities; and identifying target companies or organizations you are interested in, among others. But the most important readiness factor before beginning the job search is your psychological state.

Psychological state? Yes, your psychological state.

This might be a delicate topic for some, but I have found that the vast majority of challenges to jobseekers are issues relating to their psychological state. For nearly anyone, being in transition is painful. Sometimes it can get *real* tough—*and this is okay.* After all, we're used to a particular rhythm of life that includes work, projects, meetings, conferences, travel, and/or deadlines (not to mention pride and identity). When it comes to an abrupt halt, it's understandably upsetting.

But this upset takes a toll and can sabotage your networking and job search efforts. A sad, panicked or depressed state is not a ready state. Again, the emotional roller coaster of life is okay and natural, but taking time to deal with it is not only acceptable, but crucial. If you find that you are fearful or panicked about not finding a job (or if you have no feelings about the situation at all), it's simply too soon to begin networking. You could jump into things anyway, but mark my words when I say that it will have adverse effects on your meetings. Mental readiness is key.

Recently, I spoke with Pete, a job-seeking chief information officer. Pete reflected back on the early weeks of his unemployment and noticed in retrospect that he had felt and acted angry in some early networking situations due to losing his job. Though he may have had every right to feel angry about his situation, he made the mistake of taking that attitude into his meetings. What he found was that this affected his future efforts. While his contacts and prior job got him in the door initially, he noticed that the networking seemed to stop there. This, he came to realize, was due to the attitude. Pete isn't a bad guy, but he wasn't ready to network yet. Consequently, people took his attitude as a sign and weren't willing to risk their reputation by sending him to valuable people in their networks.

"I won't have a chance to go back and remake those first impressions," he told me. Unfortunately, he's probably right. Why make that same mistake if you can see it coming?

A while ago, I met with Jane, a job-seeking executive. Jane's manner of speaking was curt, her voice extra loud, and her gestures unusually expansive. She spoke at length about the faults of her prior employer. When I asked if perhaps she was struggling a bit with the change in her employment status, she slammed her hand on the desk. I literally jumped. Her voice was angry and the volume was high. "NO!" she yelled. She was actually shaking. I moved on to another topic, but concluded that any referrals to other networking contacts would be embarrassing for me and fruitless for her.

Now contrast Jane with Ellona, who was comfortable with her transition. While giving me her background, she explained her circumstances in a positive but matter-of-fact tone. There was no negativity or criticism of her former employer (trust me, I can make my own judgments and draw my own conclusions about such situations), and there was humor and laughter in our meeting. I actually had fun! Ellona was someone I definitely wanted to connect with my professional colleagues, and I knew that they would like her, too. Coming from a recruiter, someone whose network is her business, that's an important distinction when compared with an experience such as my meeting with Jane.

BOTTOM LINE: Take some time. Whether you are new to the working world or a seasoned professional, it takes time to get mentally ready. I don't need to tell you that it's impossible to be a confident networker when you're lacking confidence in yourself. *Be ready.*

For practice, turn to page 143 for a quick exercise that will help you assess your own readiness to get into the job market. Once you've spent some time with these questions and feel confident in your answers, come back as we dive into the framework of *The 20-Minute Networking Meeting*.

Real-World Perspective
Like He Read My Mind —
a 20-Minute Meeting

Over the course of the last year, I met with over two hundred jobseekers that ranged from new high-school grads to some of the world's most senior executives. We discussed fears, concerns, job-seeking strategies, resumes, business bios, cover letters, LinkedIn and nearly all other things job-search related. But once in a while someone will call a networking meeting that is incredibly informed, informative, brief and impactful. Here is one such case. It's a great example that shows how effective networking can help both parties.

Santi and I met at a *20-Minute Networking Meeting* presentation. Already in a professional role as a marketing lead for a small company in the Minneapolis area, Santi had landed his opportunity right out of university; an unusual thing for most new graduates. He introduced himself to me after the discussion. He made a positive impression right away. I was happy to say yes to his networking request, and we got in touch soon thereafter.

Arriving early to get some work done, I grabbed two seats and a cup of coffee. Santi arrived right on time for our appointment. He made eye contact, shook my hand, and expressed his appreciation for my time with a warm, confident smile. From that moment alone I could understand why Santi was in a leadership role so soon out of school.

Even as we settled in, Santi thanked me again for my willingness to meet. He reminded me that his purpose was to discuss international marketing and whether I might know of other professionals with that particular experience. A native of Argentina, Santiago (Santi) was weighing an opportunity in South America that would utilize his marketing background, bilingual abilities, and international experience thus far. Due to my work with executives, he asked, did I know of someone with a similar background that he could talk to?

On the spot, I couldn't think of anyone. But seeing that he would conduct this kind of meeting with anyone I introduced him to, I told him that I'd be in touch when someone came to mind.

Having addressed his networking request right up front, we moved onto other topics. While I had a few things to talk about, I was curious to know how Santi got his current role so quickly out of college.

The answer? Networking.

An enthusiastic student of marketing, Santi has a willingness to help people and to expand his personal experiences. By the time he had graduated, he had been meeting the right people at the right times for months, and, always armed with confidence and a smile, the opportunity nearly found *him*.

Then Santi was thanking me again. Not wanting to take up too much time, and needing to get back to work, he began to collect his things. But not before asking how he could help me too.

As chance would have it, I was in search of professionals for two boards of directors that I was serving on. I described what I was looking for. Not able to think of people right off hand, Santi said that he too would get back to me soon.

We stood and shook hands. All done. Even though our conversation changed track a couple of times, we still came in around twenty minutes. It was fun, efficient, and helpful to us both. Not only that, but once I reached out to him with some people that I thought could assist his networking, Santi then sent me the contact information for no less than ten people that fit the boards of directors descriptions that I was looking for. Talk about win-win! Success for both sides!

Your 20-Minute Networking Meeting Cheat Sheet

All right, now we're rollin'. Here's a very brief overview of what's coming. This cheat sheet will be available again at the end of the book for easy reference. (See page 142.)

Note the time frames for each step. *The 20-Minute Networking Meeting* is really this simple. It consists of five parts:

STEP 1:	**Great First Impression**	2–3 minutes
STEP 2:	**Great Overview**	1 minute
STEP 3:	**Great Discussion**	12–15 minutes
STEP 4:	**Great Ending**	2 minutes
STEP 5:	**Great Follow-Up**	After the Meeting

And that's it!

Each one of these steps will be detailed in the pages to come, letting you know what to do, how to do it, and why.

FIRST UP: STEP 1 — Great First Impression

Step 1—
Great First Impression

GOAL:	To make a great first impression
HOW:	With thanks and short chitchat
TIME LIMIT:	2 to 3 minutes
WHAT YOU WILL DO:	Arrive, express gratitude, highlight connections, set the agenda
NOTE:	Turn to page 147 for your Great First Impression Planner

ARRIVING FOR YOUR 20-MINUTE NETWORKING MEETING

Arrive a few minutes early. If you're meeting at a coffee shop or restaurant, arrive as early as you'd like. If you're meeting at your contact's place of business (I'm speaking from experience here), don't arrive too early.

THE REASON: If you're meeting at a public place, you can do as you please. But if you're meeting at your contact's workplace, it can be uncomfortable for them to know that someone is waiting—especially if he or she has work to do before the meeting. In the past, I've had guests arrive up to forty-five minutes early. It's not my habit to keep guests waiting, but giving up lunch or a much needed break to start a meeting way ahead of the scheduled time isn't exactly something most people care to do either. It can result in a meeting with a distracted or annoyed contact.

WHAT TO DO: If you find yourself with extra time, find a place to sit and work outside the office. Review your notes for your meeting. Take a stroll around the block to collect your thoughts. Maybe you'll even see something interesting to talk about in your meeting.

Here are some other things to concern yourself with until your appointment:

- Double check: Do you have your resume, pen, and notebook?
- Are you prepared for the questions and topics that you wish to discuss?
- If you're in the office, take a look around. What do your surroundings tell you about this organization and its culture?

<><><><><><><><><><><><><><><><><><><><><><><><><><><><><><><><><><><><><>

TIP:
Familiarizing yourself with your environment will help
you feel more comfortable before your networking
meeting. It may even provide some informal conversation
as you begin your networking discussion.
Take a look around!

<><><><><><><><><><><><><><><><><><><><><><><><><><><><><><><><><><><><><>

Don't be fooled. Your first impression starts the moment
you arrive for your meeting. Be respectful toward anybody who greets you (assistants, front desk people). This
is essential to remember because often your contact will
ask their opinion of you. ("Was she friendly? Courteous?
Appreciative?")

EXPRESSING GRATITUDE

Before there is any networking discussion, share a hearty smile
and a firm handshake during your introduction. And look your
contact in the eye. You'd be surprised how often I get feedback
from clients telling me that even executive candidates have inade-
quate eye contact. A shy or nervous professional can leave the
impression of inexperience. That would suggest that you're not
ready for a networking meeting. And if you're not ready for a
meeting, why would you be ready for the professional world?

Once you get a lock on your introduction, express your gratitude. Perhaps you already thanked your contact by email or over
the phone when you set up the meeting, but it's always necessary
to offer thanks again.

THE REASON: Remember—this person is giving you the *gift*
of time. Acknowledging that fact in a sincere manner will earn
you a lot of respect and gratitude in return. As far as how to
express your thanks, you can do that any way you'd like. But here
are a few examples to start with.

"It's great to see you, Jack. Thank you again for meeting with me."

"Nice to meet you, Carroll. I really appreciate your time today."

"Hi, Emily! What a great office! Again, thank you for agreeing to see me."

As you can tell, it doesn't have to be anything too fancy; it's simply the thought that counts.

All right, so now you have a grip on introductions. Next . . .

HIGHLIGHT CONNECTIONS

Though your meeting may start with a little small talk around the artwork in the lobby or the scenery you saw outside, a better way toward a great impression is by highlighting mutual connections.

THE REASON: If you don't know the person you are meeting with all that well, it can be a safe way to bridge the gap. People feel more comfortable knowing that they have acquaintances in common. And there are many ways to make this connection, so don't worry if you don't have a close connection to your contact.

WHAT TO DO:

- Remind the other person of who connected you in the first place:
  "Cindy Arabella asked to send her greetings. Cindy has been a great help to me, and she said you were a great help to her."

- Mention other people you know in common:
  "I think we might have people in common at Skyline

Hauling. Do you know Milo Marks or Tommy Bennett?"

If it seems you have no one in common (because you connected with someone via email, for instance), you can try these approaches:

- Suggest other likely professional connections:
  "I think we both volunteer at the local humane society."

- Ask about a person you both may know (but only if you think it is likely; don't do this just for sake of banter):
  "You're a member of Front Range Ski Club in Loveland? Do you happen to know Connor Cooper?"

Or, if appropriate, you could make a personal connection. (By appropriate, I mean that crossing personal boundaries could come across as creepy and make your contact uncomfortable.)

"Your website bio mentioned that you live in Wellesville. I grew up in nearby Millerton before heading to college."

Or:

"I read that you're an alum of Ashbury College. My sister got her undergraduate degree at Ashbury 5 years ago."

TO REPEAT: You should use the last example only if you believe it would be well received. Taking your professional networking meeting into the personal realm can be a powerful tool, but it can backfire easily if your contact does not care to discuss anything other than business.

At this point, you now have your introductions and expression of gratitude behind you. What's next? Getting to the point. (And feel free to state you're doing so!)

SETTING THE AGENDA

Here it is—the moment of (literal) truth. Tell your contact you're only going to take twenty minutes, and share exactly what you're hoping to talk about in that time.

THE REASON: As you've already read in this book, most people expect a networking meeting to take an hour. Even when someone says, "Really, just a few minutes of your time." However, you can reaffirm your promise by laying out an actual agenda ahead of time. This will help your contact believe that you'll keep to your promise of twenty minutes.

Here are a few more reasons why setting the agenda is important.

It will set the tone of:

- The meeting
- The impression you create
- Your overall job-search approach

In addition, it will show that you are:

- Prepared
- Considerate of your contact's time
- Unafraid to lead

WHAT TO DO: Introductions and gratitude out of the way, hit the seats and start the meeting by stating your intent, and conveying that you only need a small amount of their time.

REMEMBER: The person is doing you the courtesy of meeting with you. Return the courtesy by acknowledging that fact.

Let's see what a couple of examples would look like (and don't worry—you don't have to get too fancy with this, either):

"Thanks again for meeting with me, Tessa. I just need twenty minutes. I want to give you a brief overview of my background and ask a few questions that help in my job search."

"This will be brief, Fiona. I just hope to mention a few of my academic and professional highlights and get your perspective on a few things that relate to my job search."

And that's it. Really! If you care to be a little more specific, you can do so. But keep it short and crisp, and stick with the two to three-minutes you have for this step.

REAL-WORLD PERSPECTIVE

Customer service rep Dan used the principles of *The 20-Minute Networking Meeting* in his job search. When asked what part of the *20MNM* proved most valuable in his meetings, he had this to say.

"It was having an agenda that I could follow. If my meeting got off track, or if one of us went on a tangent, I always knew what part of the agenda was next. That kept things moving and on track."

When asked why this was significant, he said, "Because I always knew what to say next, and I think that leaves a good impression."

A VERY IMPORTANT SIDE NOTE:

Though it is important to make your agenda clear, please remember that you *do* have flexibility if you need it. I know I've expressed this notion before, but if your introduction goes well and your chitchat extends past your first two minutes, that's *totally okay!* But be sensitive—if your chatting goes for five minutes or more, do your best to get things back on track and not overstay your welcome. The only exception here is if your contact is leading your talk.

IMPORTANT:

Don't wait for your contact to start the discussion. You called the meeting and it is your responsibility to manage it. After all, would you agree to attend a meeting called by someone else and then be expected to run it yourself? Probably not. Be the professional that you are and lead!

REAL-WORLD PERSPECTIVE — WHERE IS THE AGENDA?

A job-seeking executive came in for a meeting and plopped down in the chair across from me. We exchanged a few pleasantries, and then . . . nothing. No agenda, no plan for the meeting. At the time, I was writing this very book on effective networking. Because it was not my responsibility to lead this person's meeting, I let the awkward silence play out, wondering if this executive, previously in a chief executive officer role, would catch on and grab hold of the meeting. He did not. A number of explanations strolled through my mind, but it struck me as strange that a CEO would ask for a meeting and expect me (or some other person) to run it. It did not leave me with a good impression.

In the end, I found a way to participate in the meeting anyway, and even gave the person a helpful suggestion or two. But I did not offer any networking names. My thought was that if I sent him to any of my contacts, he would conduct himself the same way. My contacts are too important to me, and I could not have them thinking I endorse such behavior. Bound by that fear, I was forced to play it safe, and meted out only minimal assistance. I know by experience that this jobseeker left our meeting with some sense of "success," having networked and gained a couple of tips. But he lost the chance to get some meaningful contacts, and certainly to gain an evangelist.

Why didn't I help him more? Why didn't I take the time to teach him how to conduct a networking meeting?

The answer is simple: It's not a professional service for offer. There are, in fact, outplacement consultants and career coaches who work with jobseekers to help them plan and execute their job search.

The people you are networking with are not likely to be professional job coaches and resume writers. That is not their job. It is *your* job to have the right resources to help you frame up your job search. And certainly don't expect them to set the agenda for your meeting, either. *You're* in control of the meeting. Take charge!

Step 2 —
Great Overview

GOAL:	Give a great overview of your background
HOW:	Providing a crisp, brief, and memorable understanding of your work experience
TIME LIMIT:	1 minute (You want to leave time for your Great Discussion!)
WHAT YOU WILL DO:	Briefly state your experience
NOTE:	Turn to page 150 for your One-Minute Overview Planner

BREAKING DOWN YOUR ONE MINUTE

Right about here you're probably reeling over "one minute."

"Whoa, whoa," you say. "But I've got 30 years of experience! How can I cram all of that in one minute?"

Or perhaps you have a limited amount of experience and are wondering if you have *enough* to talk about. Is it even possible to create a snapshot that lasts 60 seconds?

Yes to both questions, and I'll show you exactly how. For the moment, however, we must establish why a one-minute set up of your background is crucial to your overall 20-minute discussion.

THE REASON: A one-minute overview is efficient and strategic. The objective is to provide a *general* sense of what you've done. With a clean-as-a-whistle, one-minute snapshot, your contacts can think about who to connect you with or where you "fit" job-wise when they hear of an opening.

REMEMBER: The objective of the networking meeting is to gather information, gain a contact or two, and (hopefully) create an evangelist. If you find that you have *more* than a minute's worth of material, choose carefully; you want to avoid extra details that may be irrelevant and difficult to remember. It may bog people down for this kind of meeting. (You're networking, not interviewing.) The idea is to keep things to a minimum so that you may discuss the real information you're after.

WHAT TO DO:
- Tally your years in your particular job function
- Highlight your background
- Follow with where (organizations) you've worked
- Tie those with the most recent titles you've held
- String them all together

Here they are again, with examples. (Fully written overviews will follow.)

Think number of years in the function:

"Overall, I've got twenty-three years in technical sales."

"I was in plant operations for ten years before moving into general plant management for the last twelve years."

Consider the highlights of your background:

"I made President's Club for sales excellence ten years in a row at Hewlett."

"I was rewarded for best customer service 3 years in a row."

Followed by places you've worked:

"I've been at large companies like Xerox as well as smaller distributors."

"I have worked at some of the most respected parts manufacturers in our region."

Tied in with most recent titles you've held:

"I was regional manager most recently."

"My most recent title was group lead; before that, I was support manager."

Getting a feel for it? Here are three more examples of the high-level view of information you want to share regarding your specific experiences, skills and abilities.

"I'm a twenty-year training professional specializing in truck and rig repair."

"I am a senior financial broker with a background in family financial planning."

"I have fifteen years as a private kinder-care provider, and am now in my eighth year as a geriatric professional."

Here's a tip: Your one-minute overview could also include references to any people or places that you have in common with the networking contact:

"ExCo is where I worked with our mutual friend, Obie Jones."

"I saw that you were at IBM in the last seven years. My brother was there for a few of those same years."

"I got my CPE certification in 2010, working with Jeanne McGuff. It's through her that I was connected to you."

◇◇◇

There's always flexibility in how you present yourself.
All examples are only meant to be a guideline.
If you like them, use them! If you want to put
your own flair on it, do so!

◇◇◇

REAL-WORLD PERSPECTIVE

Dave is a fellow recruiter and frequent networker. He reiterated the importance of a brief overview.

"I don't want to hear the full story of their background," he told me when I interviewed him for this book. And it's not because Dave isn't interested in hearing the person's experience.

"It's just that I don't have the time."

Dave is a really nice guy who cares about people. I know this because I know him.

"I would like to hear more," he went on, regretfully. "But I can't. These days, even the *Reader's Digest* condensed version is a little too long."

Another professional who is frequently asked to network with others shared the same sentiment but has a very different reaction to a long-winded overview.

"It's a red flag," Sharon said of a personal story that gets too long. The leader of a fast-growing professional services firm, she sees time management and self-management as a number-one priority. "And if they are too into their story, something isn't right."

BOTTOM LINE: Keep it brief, but structured. Shorten the overview. A lot. Yes, a minute is a relatively short time, but by reading the above, it should be clear how quickly, efficiently, and accurately you can describe your work history. Just practice. Rehearse. Time yourself. You will be surprised at what you can convey in just sixty seconds.

SAMPLES OF ONE-MINUTE OVERVIEWS

Here are some fully articulated One-Minute Overviews. Suggestion: Read them out loud and time them.

EXAMPLE 1— CAMERON

"Nice to meet you, Barbara. I believe you already have my resume. There's a lot more detail there, but basically I'm a professional with twenty years of experience in the public service sector. I'm currently working as a support admin at Serve the Youth, where I've been for the last five years. There I was promoted to take over my community service group. That group oversees 15 regional cities. With a staff of around fifty people in each city, Serve the Youth provides job training for at-risk youth as well as 'get started' assistance with financial planning and life skills. I support the leaders in each of those cities. Prior to joining Serve the Youth, I was senior admin of a high school remedial program in the Lodge Lake School System.

Ideally, I'd like to stay in the community service sector. My passions are for education, youth, and community development."

How did that sound? Speaking that overview out loud takes around forty-five seconds!

EXAMPLE 2— EMILIO

"Thank you again for taking the time to meet with me. I've been in consumer marketing since I got my bachelor's from Michigan State University in 2000. After five years at Highland Mills in product marketing, I went to a smaller foods manufacturer and focused on foods marketing to nontraditional channels, such as drug and discount stores, clubs, and dollar stores. I loved the nontraditional retail environment and I've stayed there ever since. The last three years, I've been part of sales and marketing with See-Go Brands, participating on a national team selling into retail and helping introduce new products in the organic foods arena. I'm ideally looking for a sales or marketing role that is consumer product based."

How about that one? Time to spare!

REMINDER: For an exercise in how to put together a one-minute overview, turn to page 150. It will walk you through the process.

Step 3 —
Great Discussion

GOAL:	Have a short but great discussion
TIME LIMIT:	12–15 minutes
WHAT YOU WILL DO:	Talk through Five Key Questions You will draft Key Questions 1–3 yourself, using *The 20-Minute Networking Meeting* structure. Then, I will tell you exactly what to ask in Question 4 and Question 5. *(We'll get to specifics in a second. Here's some prep first.)*
NOTE:	Turn to page 157 for your Great Discussion Planner

GREAT DISCUSSION

As you can deduce, most of *The 20-Minute Networking Meeting* is spent in discussion. Still, you shouldn't spend any more than fifteen minutes in this part of the meeting. Admittedly, a robust discussion can—and typically *does*—last more than twelve to fifteen minutes, but to respect the other person's schedule, and to keep to your promise, be flexible, but stay on target. The only exception is if your contact is leading the discussion, and it seems rude or counterproductive to get things back on track. In that case, just let things flow for a few extra minutes. But pay attention for signs indicating your contact is ready to wrap up the meeting!

WHAT YOU SHOULD KNOW

THIS IS IMPORTANT: During your meeting, never, under any circumstances, ask for information that you should already know. We alluded to this earlier in the book, but it bears repeating. This includes general info about your contact's company, the economy, political climate, news reports, or anything that a newspaper or the Internet could readily tell you.

THE REASON: Your contact reads the papers too and, like you, probably is aware of the business happenings in your region and the general business climate overall. But how unfortunate (embarrassing) would it be if you were completely clueless about such information (especially concerning your contact's organization)? You are there hoping to make a good impression!

On the other hand, with such busy schedules, your contacts might have far less time to learn what's happening with specific organizations, new products, up-and-coming sectors, or possibly (believe it or not) the trends happening right in his or her own industry.

Think about it—could this have been *you* at some point? Are you always familiar with the latest social networking trends, newest changes in technology or the latest happenings in the market? Do you know the thought leaders and visionaries in your profession? Probably not all the time. So why would it be any different for any other busy networking contact.

WHAT TO DO: Research. Research these categories *before-hand*—and never ask about them during the meeting:

- The overall economy and business climate
- The job market
- Political changes that affect your industry or job function
- Generally available information about your industry or job function
- Readily available information about the organization and the person you're meeting with

KNOW THE PERSON YOU'RE TALKING TO

It's extremely disappointing when someone comes to meet with me and doesn't really know who I am or what I do. Most professionals feel the same, and will pass on the opportunity to help that person. As much as possible, you should know the person you're talking to.

THE REASON: It's rude if you're unfamiliar with the person you're asking assistance from. You somehow believed they could help you, yet you know nothing about them?

One of my professional friends, Barney, is about as well-connected as they come, and as a consultant he is often asked to meet for networking. He too notices when people have not done their homework before getting together.

"If someone asks to meet with me and starts by saying, 'So, what do you do?'" he says, "Our meeting suddenly becomes awfully short!"

WHAT TO DO: More research.

Here are a few things someone would learn about me from my bio on my company website:

- My job title and specialty areas
- How long I have been with my firm
- The other jobs I have had
- My educational background
- Nonprofit boards that I serve on
- Professional memberships and certifications I have

As you can see, that's a lot of fodder for great discussion, taken directly from my company bio. And that's just from the company website alone! If the individual also checked my LinkedIn page, he or she would have learned even more, including:

- The number of years I spent at each of my previous employers, along with my actual job titles
- Some of my professional interests (i.e., what LinkedIn groups I belong to)
- How networked I am (i.e., how many people I am linked with)
- People we know in common
- Professional books I've endorsed
- People I've recommended
- And a lot more!

Now, your contact might *not* have this level of information readily available, but in the age of social media, it's rare to find absolutely nothing about your contact someplace online. Take the time to get to know the person you're meeting with.

REAL-WORLD PERSPECTIVE

Quinn is a business owner and frequent networking contact who shares my belief in the importance of good planning. When professionals don't take the time to learn who she is and what she does before a networking meeting, it's a big disappointment.

"When I meet with people, I ask them whether they have visited my company's website." When the occasional networker admits that she or he hasn't, Quinn, none too shy with her feelings or thoughts, asks, "Why not?"

The message here is obvious, but if you don't like the idea of being put on the spot, be prepared. Even Quinn hopes that by asking such a potentially embarrassing question, the networker will not make the same mistake in future meetings.

KNOW THE COMPANY

It's safe to assume that when it comes to networking, a contact's company is just as important as the contact. That's to say, help from a contact in a different industry—or from a contact at a consulting company, or from someone who is unemployed—might come in a format different than that of a peer or colleague in the same industry. But if the company is a fast-growing Fortune 500, for example, it gives a lot of weight to who your contact is and what role he or she plays in the organization. So, again, knowing about the company is just as important as knowing about your contact, regardless of the organization's size.

THE REASON: It was mentioned before, but imagine how unfortunate (embarrassing) it would be to arrive at your contact's office without knowing what the company does.

WHAT TO DO: Research. Here are some examples of things you should know. (But don't limit yourself to these!):

- Recent important events
- Press releases
- Key customers
- New product introductions
- Milestones
- Pending deals
- Positive news write-ups

HOW TO DO IT: The web is a miraculous source of information. Many company websites contain press releases that will detail recent events and even mention new customers or business relationships. They, of course, will also mention new products (if that's not the first thing you see on the website).

<><><><><><><><><><><><><><><><><><><><><><><><><><><><><><><>

With so much information readily available on the web, and with so many convenient ways to access it, there's no excuse going into a networking meeting uninformed. Do your research!

<><><><><><><><><><><><><><><><><><><><><><><><><><><><><><><>

KEEP IN MIND: The more you know, the better the impression you will leave. Now, that's not to say you need to have a night of memorization before your morning meeting, but knowing key points that are important to the organization (milestones, pending deals, positive news write-ups) can only help. Just think: How flattered would *you* be if someone came to your office knowing something meaningful about your organization, your work and the things you've helped it accomplish? Wouldn't you be more willing to help this person? (If you didn't think about it yet, you can also see how this can help create an evangelist!)

There are five questions that will provide the structure for the discussion part of your networking meeting. Before we get to them, however, we must discuss some questions that you should never ask. These are the questions that have become the boring standard in business and networking meetings. They're not necessarily deal-breakers, but they will define you as the same as any other net-worker who didn't "have the time" or put forth the effort to do some homework. Avoid these, and you will stand out in good fashion.

Here they are. (Some of these repeat things we've already talked about, but there's no hurt in re-reminding.)

- **As mentioned, do not ask questions about things you should already know.** This includes what the contact's company does, how business has been lately, things about the economy, well-known trends in your industry, and so on. You could, however, ask for your contact's reaction to something you've read or heard on a given topic. It's always good to encourage thoughts and opinions of a contact.
- **Do not ask for work history or background overview.** Your contact is not being interviewed—don't make him or her feel that way, especially if you're the one looking for work. Find out the person's background yourself!
- **Do not ask how the two of you are connected.** You should already know this. It's your responsibility to remind your contact about personal or professional connections.

- **Do not ask "What do you think about my resume?"** Unless they've offered to discuss it, it can put someone on the spot. It's also not relevant. Why? *You're* not being interviewed, either. Even a Human Resources or hiring professional would not appreciate this question, as resume review is rarely part of their job responsibilities. An appropriate person to ask for resume feedback would be an outplacement counselor or a job coach.

- **Do not ask personal questions without a purpose.** "Do you have children?" is not a suggested icebreaker. Respect the boundary between personal and professional questions.

- **Do not ask the contact to divulge any information about the organization that should not be shared in a relatively new relationship,** such as specific plans for upcoming lay-offs, upcoming product launches, personnel changes, and the like.

REAL-WORLD PERSPECTIVE

Remember Barney, my well-connected consultant friend? Barney evaluates the level of preparation a jobseeker has put into the meeting. He anticipates that the person has "pre-thought" the meeting and therefore is "able to comment on what they have learned about me, my company, my profession." The amount of preparation affects Barney's willingness to share leads and suggest other professionals to call.

"None of my connections would ever hire someone unprepared for an interview," Barney explained. "A networking meeting, to me, is a clear indicator how someone would act in a future interview."

Even if your approach would be different, would you be willing to risk that impression?

FIVE KEY QUESTIONS: QUESTIONS 1 - 3

Your first three questions are intended to guide the very important discussion portion of your networking meeting. A short, productive meeting can be difficult for many jobseekers. But with a little thought and practice, you'll not only lead your meeting but control its direction too.

So how do you have a meaningful discussion that is still clean and crisp while you're networking? By formulating your first three questions from the research you've done before the meeting.

You will create these key questions following the *20MNM* structure. What you ask will be completely up to you, but they must be constructed for the contact you're meeting with, according to your networking goals.

Why? To gain the unique wisdom or specific knowledge that you wish to learn from this particular contact. These are never questions that address common knowledge, or something that could be found during your prep work. Instead, they are thought-out, courteously asked inquiries specific to your contact that, perhaps, only your contact could answer.

Where's a good starting point for such carefully designed questions? Your contact's bio or LinkedIn profile, or even the contact's company website.

No such resource available on your contact? Then familiarize yourself with their profession so that you may ask informed questions that will ultimately inform your conversation. Read through the material carefully. The moment you wonder about something, jot it down. From here you can formulate dynamic, thought-provoking questions.

Here's such a scenario:

You're perusing your contact's LinkedIn profile and realize that she has certifications that you've considered getting. Formulating a question around this will not only give you something to talk about, but will provide a solid piece of information that will help you in the future.

HOW TO STRUCTURE THESE QUESTIONS

These specific contact questions come in two parts. The first part is an **observation** (or a piece of information), and the second part is the **related question** (or a request for comments from the contact).

Here is an example for the above scenario.

"Johanna, you have your Certificate of Clinical Competence (**observation**). *Has it been valuable in developing your Speech-Pathology career* (**related question**)?"

Make sense? You've pointed out your observation and then you've asked a thought-provoking question related to it. Here are more examples:

"You were a high school teacher, then later worked with Pre-K and toddlers (**observation**). *Looking back, would you have done it in the same order* (**related question**)?"

"You've worked as a paralegal in both the health care and insurance industries (**observation**). *How do you compare the need for legal professionals in those two sectors* (**related question**)?"

"I'd like to ask your opinion about commercial real estate management. You started with a more traditional background when entering the field (**observation**). *Is that a recommended route, or is there a way you would have done it differently* (**related question**)*?"*

"Early on, you spent ten years in maintenance and repair (**observation**). *Did you find that your experience set you up for the mechanical work you're doing now* (**related question**)*? Was there a hard lesson that you learned that could make that transition easier for me* (**related question**)*?"*

"You're also a former athlete (**observation**). *I feel I could capitalize on my team-work experience on the plant floor* (**observation**). *Do you feel that's been the case for you* (**related question**)*? How has your team-play experience impacted your professional life* (**related question**)*?"*

WHAT THE STRUCTURE DOES

Placing the *observation* at the beginning of your questions establishes the fact or point you're addressing. This gives the listener the heads-up as to where you're going. The *related question*, in turn, evokes the person's assistance, thereby sparking discussion. In simpler terms: You give a heads-up about *what* you're going to ask, then you ask for thoughts.

TIP:

Asking a second related question, as in the last two examples, is perfectly acceptable. However, it's important to remember that your meeting is not a question-answer session. Sometimes it's best (even strategic) to let your contact answer your first question before you follow up with your second question—if they didn't already answer it in the process of answering the first. This way you won't put your contact on the spot or give the impression that you have a list of questions to answer. It also helps bring more depth to your discussion by delving further into your topic.

ANOTHER TIP :

Sometimes you can reuse your great discussion questions in multiple networking meetings. This might be valuable if, for example, you would like to get more than one perspective on a matter of great interest to you in your search. You must still think carefully about the questions you select for each networking meeting. Don't ask similar questions for lack of planning!

REAL-WORLD PERSPECTIVE

Sophie is the president of a consortium of companies in the steel manufacturing industry.

"I do a fair bit of networking as part of my job leading a large trade association. My association posts some positions on our website, and I am often privy to other openings on a somewhat confidential basis.

"While I don't mind taking the meetings, I am constantly surprised by how poorly prepared some of the networkers are. People show up and are very happy about the meeting and pleasant to talk to, which seems to make the meeting go a little long. I don't have a problem with that, but I do have a problem when people arrive without a sense of who I am or what my company does. The lack of preparation renders them less able to manage the meeting effectively, and—here is my hot button—when someone requests a meeting with me and spends the time asking me about my own background, it can feel like I'm being interviewed! I wonder if these people do this in their real jobs—do they call meetings and show up unprepared and let the other person do the talking? I mean, how long would it take to do some basic planning ahead of time? Sometimes it's as though jobseekers seem to lose their ability to plan along with losing their job. It's extremely frustrating."

FIVE KEY QUESTIONS: QUESTION 4

Your fourth question will help you with a major objective for the meeting: expanding your network. Essentially, you'll be asking your contact to recommend the names of some individuals whom you can reach out to. This question will be similar each time you ask it, but slightly tailored on a case-by-case basis. The gist is to ask for further networking contacts.

This is where networking breaks down for jobseekers at all experience levels, including executives. It's where I've seen a lot of people freak out. The general consensus is: *It was hard enough asking for the meeting itself! If I ask for names of other people,*

I'm gonna seem pushy or desperate."

That's not true. That's how business works—give-and-take. Also, this feeling (and the excuses that come with it) isn't unusual, so there's nothing to worry about here. In fact, I've heard these same protests for as long as I can remember (along with, *"No one wants to give names of other people,"* and, *"This part is just too uncomfortable!"*). But not a day of business goes by when people aren't doing this very thing on every level in every industry out there. Looking at it from that standpoint, there's no reason to avoid asking the question.

Having said that, I want to acknowledge that getting started isn't all that easy. So, here are a couple of tips to deal with the fear.

- Remind yourself that the people you meet with have also had to find a job at one time too. Some more than once. They know the value of networking. They get it.
- Remind yourself that these people said *yes* to a meeting with you in the first place. They likely know that you will be asking for names of contacts.
- Because they know the drill, they may even have come prepared with some names in mind.

REAL-WORLD PERSPECTIVE

Jerlyn is a business owner who often meets with professionals in her industry. She told me that she expects a networking meeting to include a request for other contacts.

"I come prepared with some ideas," she told me. "But the 'ask' is important, too. I won't give the names without the question."

WHAT HAPPENS IF THEY SAY NO?

Well, then they say no (which is the worst that can happen). A gracious thank you will suffice, and then you simply move on to your fifth and final question.

Let's get to some examples. If the general question that you want to ask is "Who else do you know that might be a good contact for me in my job search?" you could probably go ahead and just say as much. But put a little more consideration behind it, and you might get a much better response.

Here are some ways to ask:

"Do you know of someone else with a social worker background who might answer the same questions I asked you?"

"Do you know of another groundskeeper at a different company that might be good to call?"

"You used to work for JPN. Are there any current or former community service colleagues there whom I could touch base with?"

Notice the phrasing in those questions. They're direct, yet considerate. They're not blunt, but they're totally clear. Word choice is needed. Sincerity and appreciation are crucial. But it doesn't have to be anything difficult. Just give thought to your words, and rest assured that you're not the only person who has asked them before. But again, it's your gracious attitude and genuine appreciation that will make the difference.

Years ago, I got a cold call from a sales representative in the clothing business. She asked for a few minutes of my time to come in and show me her line of custom clothing. I wasn't sure if I was the custom-clothing type, but I said yes to the meeting. At the end of the meeting, I decided that I definitely was not the custom-clothing type of person and elected not to make a purchase. The meeting had been very pleasant and the sales representative had been gracious. Undaunted, she proceeded to what we are calling Question 4, but instead of directly asking, "Who else do you know that might be interested in buying from my line of custom clothing?" she asked slightly modified ones instead. Like, "Who do you know that is interested in fashion?" "Who do you know that you would describe as 'trendy'?" "Do you have any friends who drive fancy sports cars?" Had she asked me for a straight referral, I'm not sure I would have been able to deliver one. But with questions phrased in different ways, I was able to think of several possible names. Your careful phrasing can have the same outcome.

◇◇◇

Positive networking gets additional contacts.
After a professionally managed meeting, sealed with gratitude and the proper give-and-take, your contacts will be much more likely to refer you to their own contacts.

◇◇◇

FIVE KEY QUESTIONS: QUESTION 5

Now, I know we've focused a lot on how to get what you need out of a networking meeting, but we can't lose sight of what networking really is—give-and-take. And while an entire book could be written about the give-and-take philosophy, this idea is worth repeating: Networking isn't all about you (or me). It's about *both* parties.

So, the last question you must ask in a networking meeting is:

"How can I help *you*?"

Yes, I admit that this question, given the topic of this book, might seem counterintuitive. But it's directly responsible for expanding your network and making evangelists of your contacts. In fact, it's possibly the most vital component of *The 20-Minute Networking Meeting*.

Big claims, right? Let me tell you why.

By nature, networking is something that must benefit both parties. I mean, asking to network, receiving the gift of time, and asking for new contacts without offering something in return (even with a gracious thank-you) is simply bad form. Worse, such a crime of *take, take, take* is rarely forgotten. But if you find a way to give back, you not only will be bestowed "good karma," you will demonstrate a clear indication of your consideration and appreciation for the time that was given to you. Offering to help in a reciprocal way also creates a sense of a peer relationship. That's where you want to be.

Besides standing out from the pack, here's what such consideration and appreciation could get you:

→ *Reciprocated* respect and consideration (Who doesn't want to help someone who helps *them*?)

WHICH COULD LEAD TO:

→ An *additional* networking meeting with that contact

   → A meeting in a different part of the same organization

WHICH COULD LEAD TO:

→ An additional name that your contact was reluctant to give up at first (Sometimes networking contacts question whether they want to give away names, but gratitude and appreciation tip the scale.)

WHICH COULD LEAD TO:

→ A wider network (Translation: more word of mouth about *you* in the marketplace.) Which could lead to:

→ An evangelist

→ A consulting / part-time gig

→ A great reputation as a thoughtful businessperson (Ask yourself whether you consider most people to be thoughtful businesspeople.)

→ And the best of all: a job opportunity!

SO HOW DO YOU PHRASE THE QUESTION?

By saying it directly. "How can I help *you*?"

Of course it could be phrased a few other ways too, but asking in an off-handed manner doesn't come across as sincere, nor does it suggest actual consideration. And no one is going to be sincere with you if you're not sincere with them. Just be direct and mean it. It will pay off.

WHAT IF THEY'RE TAKEN BY SURPRISE?

This is sure to happen. As I mentioned, it's rare for people to offer help in return for help, right? Be prepared by having done your research. Here are some scenarios:

"Thanks so much for the time and information you've given me, Kayla. Now, how can I help you?"

Kayla gives you a look of shock.

"Gosh, Brandon, I guess I can't think of anything at the moment."

But, you know how important it is to give, and if you have done your research, you'll know what to do.

What would that be, you ask? Read on for some possibilities:

"Well, you mentioned an interest in connecting with Tracy, my teacher assistant. She wrote a similar thesis. I would be happy to connect you two."

"You mentioned skiing earlier. My family took us a lot before college. I can send you a list of where to stay in Colorado or Utah for your next trip."

"My friend (uncle/father/mother) works in education. How about if I send over some information with childcare resources or private schools?"

"I went fishing any moment I had free time. How about if I send you a handful of web links that point out the hottest spots?"

And if there seems to be nothing you could help with right at that moment, have a backup:

"Well, Tammy, I really appreciated your time and input. If you think of anything I can help with in the future, please let me know. Still, as a token of appreciation for your time, I brought a reprint of a Land & Sea article on cartography. Maybe you'll find it interesting given your passion for traveling."

NOTE: You could only pull something like that off if you've done your research. If you don't know what's going on in your contact's organization, such a move is a lot less effective, or maybe ineffective. (Reminder: *Do your research!*)

Over the years, skilled networkers have done many things for me in return. A recent meeting actually resulted in a mutually beneficial conclusion. I offered some suggestions to the jobseeker on networking and job-search strategy. The person I was meeting with, in turn, offered me a networking contact that led to an ongoing consulting opportunity with a government agency. Win-win!

SUMMARY

No matter whom you meet with and no matter what you talk about, just be sure to end your meeting with Question 5.

Why end with it? Because it will leave your contact with a solid final impression of you should your meeting get interrupted or end early. Let that impression be one of consideration and appreciation—that you are gracious and grateful. Everyone is proud to know of such a thoughtful, considerate person, and better yet, everyone likes to help those people when possible.

REAL-WORLD PERSPECTIVE

Naomi is a public and corporate affairs leader for a Fortune 500 company. She had the following reaction when a job-seeking networker asked, "What can I do to help you?"

"I about fell out of my chair," she said. "No one had ever asked me that."

But the reciprocity, surprise, and the power of that question didn't stop there. Allowing herself to accept the offer, the networking favor was returned.

"Knowing I might be leaving in a few months due to layoffs, I asked the person if they could connect me with someone at another organization. They did."

According to Naomi many things changed after that day, including the fact that the original networker who requested to meet with Naomi, "has been a valuable part of my network ever since."

And what about now? Is anything different?

"It was such a poignant moment for me when that question was asked," that Naomi has begun the practice herself. The response she gets?

"The response is often a 'stunned silence.' And when I suggest a couple ways (to help)—sending an article, helping them connect with someone in my network—the person opens up," giving more information, and at times, additional names.

How's that for the power of offering to help in return? And that's coming from an executive whose expertise is media, government, and community communications!

THE IMPORTANCE OF GIVING

Then there's the flip side. While thinking about this book, and wanting to put its concept and message into practice, I agreed to meet with a C-level (chief executive; chief financial; chief operations, etc.) executive who requested a networking meeting with me. The person was referred by someone I respect, so I figured this was as solid a setup as I could ask for.

We made an appointment, and she arrived at the appropriate date and time. So far, so good. Then she jumped in by telling me about the types of jobs that she wanted. (Remember: networking contacts are not a grocery store, and they're not your immediate pathway to your next job. Hiring managers and recruiters operate in accordance with hiring necessities, not a candidate's hiring desires.) I looked through her resume and offered some recommendations and referrals, and very quickly, twenty minutes had elapsed.

Then, I turned the tides. I told her that, if we could, I was hoping the second part of the meeting could include helping me. I told her I was interested in some leadership programs she had attended and some executive groups she belonged to. I wanted to spend a few minutes picking her brain about those topics for my benefit.

Well, despite the fact that this was a *networking* meeting (which means it goes both ways—give-and-take, remember), the meeting stopped cold. There was a look of almost shock on her face. She hadn't even considered the idea of mutuality or helping the other person. I kept my own questions brief, and the discussion continued cordially. But I learned something that day. Many folks who network have still not picked up on the concept of giving back. My suggestion: Be different. Bring an attitude of helpfulness.

Turn to page 153 for examples of some actual items you might give as a token of your gratitude.

Step 4 — Great Ending

GOAL:	Make a great final impression
TIME LIMIT:	2 minutes
WHAT YOU WILL DO:	Review any action, express more gratitude, *wrap it up*!

GREAT ENDING

Every great beginning has a great ending. Now that you have reviewed your background with your contact, managed the robust discussion between the two of you, and found a way to be helpful in return, you're ready to conclude the meeting. What's most important in this case is doing so in a clear manner.

REMINDER: Your 20-minute networking meeting is probably shorter than what your contact was prepared for, which is to say that your contact, while appreciating your meeting management skills, still might be expecting a longer session. Be clear when the meeting is done.

Here are some examples:

"That's all I have to ask. Thanks again, Charles, for your time. I'm grateful for your thoughts."

"Well, I will let you get back to your workday, Freya. Thanks so much for meeting with me."

"My time is up, Paige. You've been so gracious. Thank you."

Just like any of the past examples, these wrap-ups can be modified to fit your style, so long as you hit the most critical point: showing your gratitude and sincere appreciation.

HOW TO DO IT

There are two quick steps to the great ending: recapping what you and your contact will do next, and saying *thank you* a final time.

FIRST: REVIEW ACTIONS

After you indicate that you are ending the meeting, you'll want to review any actions or next steps from the session. It'll sound something like these:

"Thank you for offering to introduce me to Nolan, I look forward to meeting him. Once I'm back at my computer, I'll send you the Events and Training calendar for the Legal Aid conference."

"Okay, I'll introduce you to Mikkal Palmer over email first thing in the morning. I hope you two can connect, as he knows a lot about the agriculture business. And, I look forward to meeting with your division hiring manager, Monica. Thanks again for setting that up."

"Well, to recap: I'll send an email with Dr. Myer's information and will forward the resume of the technician that I

think would be great for your project work. And, I really
am grateful that you will keep your eyes and ears open for
jobs or contract assignments for me."

Notice that they all express gratitude and address "next steps." Also note that they are clear indicators that the end of the meeting has come.

SECOND: EXPRESS MORE GRATITUDE

I know I've mentioned gratitude a lot over the course of this book, but I often find that it is critically undervalued. Please don't make this mistake. People appreciate being appreciated. And in the end, it will matter.

Here are some things that you'll probably be thankful for:

- Their expertise
- Their time
- Their wisdom
- Their suggestions
- Their willingness to help you at all

How about a few examples in expressing more gratitude?

"Wow, Simona Wall said you were helpful in her job
search, but the advice you gave me is invaluable. Thank
you for all that you shared with me about the recruitment
process here. I learned a ton."

"I value your wisdom, Felix. You gave me some tough
things to think about. Those thoughts will make me a bet-
ter candidate when a job opportunity opens for me. Thanks
again."

"Melanie, I see we went over by ten minutes but thank you

for the extra time. What a coincidence that there is another plant opening near my town. I will follow up with a fresh resume in two weeks."

REAL-WORLD PERSPECTIVE

Networker Joel learned *The 20-Minute Networking Meeting* model and has added a new emphasis on gratitude and humility.

"My meetings went up a notch, to an eight or nine, just by being grateful," he explained after I asked how his new approach was working for him. "I put more focus on it now. Expressing appreciation to the person for their time and the interruption in their day seems to be well received. So does thanking them for their ideas, their attention—just about everything that seems relevant."

Since then, Joel has said that he has seen this pay off in more contacts and robust relationships with the networking contacts after the initial meetings.

"They can see that I get it," he said, referring to their networking together. "And that counts for a lot."

WRAP-UP

While we've made clear that you have a lot to cover in a good wrap-up, that doesn't mean it should turn into a long goodbye. Remember, leave them wanting more. A brief but positive goodbye is all you need. Then you're set!

Step 5 — Great Follow-Up

GOAL:	Follow up after the meeting
TIME LIMIT:	Varies
WHAT YOU WILL DO:	Take prompt action to follow up after the meeting
NOTE:	Turn to page 161 for your Great Follow-Up Tracker

GREAT FOLLOW-UP

We're nearly at the end of our networking journey together. Even so, these final pages should not be overlooked. They are as vitally important as the networking meeting itself.

Following up is yet another way to show appreciation for your contact's gift of time. Equally important, it's also a way to keep your networking relationship alive. Here's a look at what's involved.

WHAT TO DO: You should keep track of everything. *Everything.*

THE REASON: Keeping track of everything (by keeping excellent notes) will allow you to back-reference your conversations, your communications, and any pertinent points of information that you should mention in your follow-up. Specific messages are far more appreciated than a simple thank-you and signature. Why? Because it leaves an impression of sincerity that you took your networking meeting to heart. Your notes will also help make your follow-up faster and more efficient. With everything already jotted down, you won't have to search your mind for thoughtful things to address, wouldn't you say?

◇◇

Keep track of *everything*. A solid set of notes will help you back-reference any pertinent points of information that you should mention in your follow-up. It builds trust and a sense of reliability. Plus, it's faster and more efficient.

◇◇

Here are some examples of what to keep track of. Be sure to write these things down the moment they happen!

- **Your phone calls.** If you speak with a contact by phone, write down the person's name and what you talked about (and that it was by phone). Keep track of things that strike you as important, new, or informative to your job search.
- **Your meeting dates.** Always be able to reference when you met, with whom you met, and what you talked about.
- **All correspondence.** Include time of original contact and responses.
- **Your follow-up messages.** (Yes, even your follow-up messages.) You should be able to look back at your notes and know each time that you have followed up. Keeping track

of your messages will also help you maintain a timeline of correspondence. This will help you gauge when it's appropriate to reach out again in the future.

- **All other pertinent information** that you've learned along the way. Sometimes someone will say something that really sticks out to you. There's no better way to make an evangelist out of a contact than having such small, but pertinent points, quotes, or pieces of information at your fingertips.

Here are some common pitfalls to avoid:

"I will be employed soon. There won't be much need for follow-up because I will be in a job before you know it."

WHY TO AVOID THIS MENTALITY: Though this could be the case, what if it doesn't happen as quickly as you expect? Besides, for any number of reasons (such as career growth, career transition, industry change, personal circumstances), you may very well want this written information months, even years down the line.

"I've got a good memory. I don't need to track my follow-up communications, because I'll just remember it all."

WHY TO AVOID THIS MENTALITY: Networking can involve scores or even hundreds of people. Remembering dates, locations, topics, mutual connections, and personal or professional interests is going to become a major issue. Don't forget, when you meet a contact, all that person has to remember is *you* (which will be easy if you have a successful first meeting). How embarrassing would it be if you can't remember that person's suggestions and advice? Worse, if you can't remember the *person*?

"I'm more of a spontaneous worker. I'll just follow up on the fly."

WHY TO AVOID THIS MENTALITY: Forgetting information or to follow up with a contact is just bad practice. Worse, it can damage trust and others' sense of your reliability. Instead, reinforce the positive impression that you create in your meetings by letting your contacts see that you're taking notes. It will build trust, and that, along with reliability, is what makes evangelists.

SPECIAL NOTE: When taking notes, consider using a notepad. Avoid the misperception that you're focused on something else when using a device.

REAL-WORLD PERSPECTIVE

A busy company owner I know takes time frequently to meet with professionals in transition. He appreciates getting a follow-up message right away.

"It is shocking to me that follow-up is often so slow," he told me, frustrated with each networking meeting that ends with no follow-up communication. "If I've set aside an amount of time to network with someone, I would hope that they could set aside enough time to follow up—and not after two weeks!"

THE KINDS OF FOLLOW-UP

Believe it or not, there are two kinds of follow-up. First, we'll deal with the immediate follow-up, and then we'll focus some attention on ongoing follow-up.

IMMEDIATE FOLLOW-UP

- First person to follow up with:
  the networking contact you just met with
- Second person to follow up with:
  the networking contact who referred you

HOW TO FOLLOW UP: By sending a thank-you. A handwritten note is always preferred, but an email will work too, so long as you do either one right away.

Here is an example of a follow-up note to a networking contact:

Dear Abigail,

It was nice to meet you yesterday. I appreciate your advice on my job search strategy with small companies and your perspective on the food service business.

Congratulations on the success your company has had this year—it was great to hear about its ten-year anniversary!

I'll let you know about the next food-and-drink session I attend.

Kind regards,
Ella Harper

And another:

Dear Jacob,

Thank you for meeting with me on September 6th. Your suggestions have already been really helpful—thank you for that, too.

As I mentioned, there's a get-together at Louie's with other custodial staff. Please be my guest. If not, I will be in touch if I run into Hal like you said I might.

Thanks again,
Footie Parker

YOUR REFERRING CONTACT

Thanking your contacts is always a must-do, but sending gratitude to the contact who referred you to your new contact is also very important. Considering this is how a network is expanded, and ultimately how work is obtained, it's an essential part of the chain. Never forget to loop back to your referring contact with a thank-you for the introduction to your new contact!

Here is an example of a thank-you message addressed to your referring contact:

Dear Hannah,

Thank you so much for connecting me to Lawrence McKeen. We met yesterday and just as you said, Lawrence (Larry) had a mountain of information about rail yards. Switch repair, here I come.

Anyway, I really appreciated the chance to meet with you and Larry and am grateful for your time and input. Hopefully we'll meet up again soon. In the meantime, please let me know if there is anything I can do for you.

All the best,
Davis Thompson

Here's another example:

Dear Mandy,

Thank you for the e-mail introduction to Christy Scott. We met for coffee yesterday. Christy's interior design back-ground is similar to the career path I hope to follow, and I feel like I'm off to a running start. Better yet, I will be meeting two of her contacts who have followed a similar journey! I couldn't have made those connections without your introduction to Christy.

I look forward to seeing you soon. You mentioned valuing input on where to find Interior Design courses for your daughter. Don't hesitate to let me know if I can help.

Kind regards,
Allie Green

◇◇

Don't let more than twenty-four hours pass
before sending a thank-you follow-up.
Much longer makes it seem like an afterthought!

◇◇

ONGOING FOLLOW-UP

So, what is ongoing follow-up if not continued contact? Well, it's actually networking maintenance. Many times, networkers send their thanks and gratitude and think that's that. This is acceptable, but it doesn't help expand or strengthen their network. And if you've noted anything by now, it's that a healthy, vibrant network is essential to business success.

WHAT TO DO: If you have meaningful reasons to check back or update a contact or contacts, then do so!

But how does one *continue* to follow up, you ask? And how often is appropriate? These are common questions, and the answers are pretty straightforward. Read on.

WHEN TO BE IN TOUCH

- **If you find an article or website** that you genuinely think the person would value. Don't ever forward something meaningless just to send a follow-up message. It can backfire. But thoughtful information, sent with good wishes and a brief update, is welcome.
- **If your contact information has changed.** If you have moved or have a new phone number or email address, you should reconnect with your network to inform them of the change. Attach an updated resume to an email message if you are still in job-search.
- **If your employment status has changed,** or if you have completed a degree or earned a significant certification. Again, you should attach an updated resume if you are still in job-search.
- **If you** *don't* **have an update that includes time-sensitive or significant information,** stay in touch about once a quarter, at most. Every few weeks is too often!

Examples:

Morgan,

Thanks again for meeting with me a few months back, and for being a part of my network. I wanted to update you that I (finally!) got my Class D driving license. Attached is my updated resume reflecting the change. If you hear of any food trucking companies looking to hire, or if I can help you in any way, please let me know.

Enjoy the weather this weekend!
Zander

Additional reasons for ongoing follow-up:

- **If you are thinking about the person and want to say hello.** Sometimes a nicely worded message to say hi is okay, but it should not be done too often; it can be received more as social or even bothersome and not professional. Use judgment.

- **If your networking introduces you to someone** who is closely connected with your contact. People enjoy it when a mutual connection is shared. When the world becomes smaller, trust is built. A word of advice, though: you should be sure about the relationship. I've had plenty of people call me and proudly tell me that they were referred to me by a "friend" of mine. Unfortunately, I frequently don't know the supposed "friend" who has connected us.

- **If you want to further discuss something mentioned in the meeting.** Perhaps your meeting revealed that you and your contact are both watching a certain start-up company or the publication of a new book by an author in your field.

How about:

Kira,

Thanks again for meeting with me last fall. I hope you had a great holiday season. In case you didn't catch this article about exotic pets in the PetVet Sentinel, I've attached a copy. Just as we discussed. They are developing a state-wide watch program!

Your advice was much appreciated and has continued to help my job search. Thank you again. Please let me know if I can ever be of assistance to you!

John Mikel Abramov

One more:

- **If you have news to share** about someone you both know (a promotion, new company, an award, etc.).

Megan,

It was great getting coffee with you last week. I am entering final interviews with two companies—I believe one of them is going to happen! Anyway, I wanted to let you know that your former co-worker Mae, who referred me to you as a networking contact, has won the Regional Small Business Award. I'm sending along a flyer about the celebration in case you hadn't received one. Maybe I will see you there!

Kind regards,
Kaydeen Sanchez

〰〰〰〰〰〰〰〰〰〰〰〰〰〰〰〰〰〰〰〰〰〰〰〰

Unless you have an update including time-sensitive or significant information, consider staying in touch about once a quarter, at most. Every few weeks is too often!

〰〰〰〰〰〰〰〰〰〰〰〰〰〰〰〰〰〰〰〰〰〰〰〰

THE KIND OF FOLLOW-UP YOU *DON'T* DO

- **Mass emails** where the email addresses of all parties are visible. (This one is horrible. It is impersonal. It also shows just how many people you're not taking seriously.) Instead, take the time to personalize each message. After all, people have networked with you one-on-one, so stay in touch in the same way.
- **Too-frequent updates** with only minuscule changes in your situation to report.
- **Stories, quotes, or platitudes** about general topics. Some job-searchers who have run out of meaningful professional updates turn to sending generic bits about leadership or business strategy, hoping that they will be noticed and remembered. After a fashion, these types of messages, if not automatically deleted, are remembered for the wrong reasons.

Most of us value meaningful updates from people we know. Recruiters and hiring professionals are no different. We share pertinent information about people among ourselves and put the most current information into our database. On the other hand, we joke about the silly, meaningless updates we get from other folks, too. How would *you* react to a weekly email from a job-seeker containing jokes, song lyrics, philosophical quotes, ditties, and the like?

EXAMPLES OF GOOD AND BAD FOLLOW-UP

First, a good follow-up message:

Hi Roberto,

Thanks again for meeting with me last month. I hope you are enjoying spring!

How about this for a coincidence? I connected with your former co-worker, Albert Nuñez, at an event for veterans. I was there with a friend who has done work with the VFW over the years. He told me that they're creating a job-search program for old and new vets, and asked me to send you his greetings.

I hope our paths cross again soon. In the meantime, please don't hesitate to let me know if I can ever help you. You were amazingly helpful to me.

Best regards,
Bobby Venter

Here's an example of a bad follow-up message:

Hey everyone,

I still haven't found a job yet. Keep me in mind if you hear of openings for bartender, restaurant manager, retail clerk, sales associate, call center associate or anything that pays decently. No painting or physical labor. Or forward my resume to others who can help.

Thanks for doing this for me!

Yondo Bondo

Another bad follow-up message:

To: *Mailing List*
Subject: *Gabby's Gallant Words of the Wise, Volume XII*

I know it's been a month since I've written, but here's your thoughts for April.

"The way to do is to be." —Lao Tzu

"People should not consider so much what they are to do, as what they are." —Meister Eckhart

I'm thinking about a lot these days and I hope you're thinking of me!

Sincerely,
Gabby Chatsworth

And of course, what will happen if you don't follow up at all: This might sound harsh, but you'll be forgotten. If you don't stay in touch in some way, people will assume you have landed in a new job and will not continue to think of you. But again, what you don't want to do is follow up so frequently that you become a bother. It's about balance. People who have taken the time to meet with you are people who care about you. Honor both their time and their concern with meaningful, occasional updates.

REAL-WORLD PERSPECTIVE

Jim is a business unit president at a large manufacturing corporation. When asked why he stopped accepting networking requests, this is what he had to say.

"I got sick of feeling used. I work for a company that has been voted one of our state's best places to work for five years in a row.

It is totally understandable why people would want to network their way into our company.

"But here's what has bothered me. I would take the time to meet with people, then I would never hear another word. Nothing. No thank-you, no follow-up, no nothing. The worst part is seeing a notice on LinkedIn or a trade publication that the person landed in a new job months ago, and me not knowing anything about it. I'd like to feel that my small contribution somehow helped them land in a job. Maybe that's just conceit. But how long does it take to send a quick email thanking people? How long does it take to prepare and send an announcement? How long to call with a message? Certainly, less time than I took for a meeting to help you when you needed it!

"Sorry to be so rigid about it. But that is my experience. I have heard the same from other execs at my company. So I quit accepting these meetings altogether. I refer callers to our HR department instead."

Pulling It All Together

At this point, you should be able to see ways to put the *20MNM* into practice for your own job search. Stick with it and have faith. We have seen these techniques used and have witnessed the amazing results for people who have been in the working world for quite some time. Better meetings, better impressions, more evangelists, more opportunities, better and sooner employment.

As we cruise the home stretch, let's look at one such professional. Ione, an administrative vice president is a convert to *The 20-Minute Networking Meeting* concepts. One of the very first to try out the *20MNM*, we thought it might be valuable to include her thoughts about how *20MNM* the model has impacted such a successful, experienced executive. Here is how she responded when I asked how the model has changed her networking:

"Overall, it has worked great! It's been far easier than I thought it would be."

Hoping for more specifics, I asked her what she had done differently than in the past.

"When I got to a meeting, instead of just jumping right in, I started by reminding the person who I was and how we were connected.

In some cases, it had been several weeks since we had set up the meeting, and I couldn't really expect people to remember who had referred me. That was a smart move. Reminding them was helpful, as they didn't seem to have a starting point with me until that moment. What I noticed is that it kick-started my conversations because we suddenly had something to talk about."

What next?
"It took some practice, but now I'm better at keeping the ball rolling. In meetings, I go over my background with much less detail than I used to. Less is more! I got more attention, more relevant questions, more thoughtful discussion."

I asked Ione why she thought that was.
"I think it was just easier for my contacts to keep track of my career path. At first, I thought I would feel cheated by a more abbreviated discussion time, but keeping it brief seemed to pay off much more. I think that was because it left room for discussion about what I had briefed them on. The expanded discussions told me I was making a better impression."

I asked what else was different from what she'd done before.
"Asking for additional contacts. I do that now. I hated the idea of doing it at first, and it's still a little strange, but no one seems surprised. I mean—it's networking. These days, I don't shy away from the question at all. Every networking meeting has generated about three new contact names, I would say, which of course results in more meetings and more names. My network has expanded exponentially, and I feel like I'm really 'getting the lay of the land' when it comes to my industry. In fact, because of this, it has even changed my thoughts about my career path, mostly because of what I've learned along the way. I couldn't have done

that without so many conversations about the market and getting so many diverse perspectives—all for asking for more people to talk with."

How do the meetings end? I wondered if that was any different.
"It's quick now. I used to say long goodbyes. I think that's because I felt so indebted for their time. But now my wrap-up is confident and succinct. I've realized this has also been well received. Maybe because it leaves the impression that I'm sensitive to the person's time. Someone even told me they wished everyone could 'stick to the ropes' the way I had."

And the follow-up?
"I try to get it done right away. It feels like if I wait more than a day, my follow-up could come across like an after-thought. I don't want to risk that."

What do you do for the follow-up?
"It's usually an email, but sometimes I send a greeting card or small gift, if the person was particularly helpful. But most importantly, I just follow up quickly."

I asked whether anyone had commented on how she approached the networking meeting.
"Actually, after my last networking meeting, the person I was sitting with commented on how well I had managed our time together. To think that I used to take more time than this. And to think I've sat with people who took more time than twenty minutes. It's just a lot easier this way. And much more appreciated."

One Final Example

A Sample 20-Minute Networking Meeting

Let's take one last look at the principles of *The 20-Minute Networking Meeting* in action. The following pages contain a full example of what a networking meeting looks like. Of course, your meetings won't go exactly as this one does, but you'll get the gist of how things might work and, more importantly, why they work that way!

We'll follow the example with imagined Q&A sheets with our imaginary characters and give example takeaways that point out the lessons. Enjoy!

SAMPLE 20-MINUTE NETWORKING MEETING

The following scenario shows the networking interaction between Bret Abrams, who was recently laid off, and Lloyd Timmins, a professional whom Bret runs into at a veterans career services event.

Bret Abrams & Lloyd Timmins

Bret pushed back his chair and stood. The main event was closing down. Time to meet people. The quarterly veterans event always had great speakers and he was glad he attended, but like the past two events, his nerves were acting up and pride was getting in the way. While he really needed a job, he just wasn't feeling social. Not tonight anyway. He gathered his things and headed for the door.

As Bret left the conference room, someone called his name. Behind him was Lloyd Timmins. Lloyd was a funny guy, a big supporter of veteran events, and one of his aunt's former co-workers. As Lloyd used to live in their neighborhood, he had been to many of their family get-togethers over the years. But it had been a while.

"Hey there, Sergeant Abrams," Lloyd said with a wry smile. They shook hands. "How's the job search going?"

Bret still wasn't comfortable talking about this.

"Pretty good," he replied. But it wasn't, and not having work yet was eating at him. Bret had lost his most recent job just eighteen months after leaving the Army, and now he was back to square one. Wanting to take the summer off before jumping back in the job market, he was feeling behind. Now he was regretting it.

"Anything promising?" Lloyd asked as they walked through the building.

It was as good a time as any. It had never been easy for Bret to ask for help, but fortune wasn't going to just drop in his lap.

"Not yet," Bret replied. "But I'm beginning to network. Like coming here." Now came the hard part. "And I'd actually really value your opinions if you have some time. Just twenty minutes."

Bret stopped at the front door. He thought he saw apprehension in Lloyd's reflection off the window, but it wasn't there when he turned.

"Twenty minutes? Geez, we can talk longer than that, Bret."

"You with work, me finding work, we're all busy. Just twenty minutes. No more."

Lloyd smiled. This was new. Bret used to be pretty shy. But Lloyd always saw the promise in him—everybody did—and he was more than happy to help.

"Of course! Let's set up a time," Lloyd said. He reached for the door handle. Then: "I don't know if you recall, but I was in your exact position this time last year."

Bret felt his eyebrows rise. Being so caught up in his own circumstances, he had completely forgotten about that. Looking back, he recalled Lloyd having a pretty tough time finding a job. Come to think of it, that's why he hadn't seen him in months.

The thought gave Bret a slight sense of relief, even a feeling of hope. If a former vet and experienced professional like Lloyd had gone through a tough job-hunt, then it wasn't just him. Lloyd would have a lot to offer when they met up again.

"I appreciate it, Lloyd. I really do. I'll send you an email to set things up."

If I'd known it was this simple, Bret thought as he left the building, I'd have started weeks ago. Better late than never.

Two weeks later, Bret arrived at Lloyd's building with plenty to talk about. It seemed inconceivable to show up asking for leads with no ideas of his own, so he had done his research.

Don't make Lloyd run the meeting, he reminded himself. You're the one looking for a job.

"Come on in!" Lloyd said, greeting him in the lobby. They

shook hands. Lloyd gestured toward a nearby breakroom, and Bret followed. He couldn't recall Lloyd being this enthusiastic or happy, even when he worked with his aunt. Something had gone right since last year.

Bret put his belongings on the table and took a seat. He respected Lloyd's busy schedule, and did not want to waste his time. He began right away.

"Thanks again for meeting with me, Lloyd. I appreciate it. And as I said, I only need 20 minutes."

"No problem. It's great to see you. Besides, I want to hear how things have been going. And your aunt, by the way, how is she?"

Lloyd explained that it was Maryam, Bret's aunt, who was coincidentally responsible for the work he was doing now. She had connected him to a set of friends that had led to the job.

This gave Bret a renewed sense of positivity. It was encouraging to know that it happened by meeting other people.

Telling himself to keep to his promise of twenty minutes, Bret got back to his agenda. *Use time wisely*, he reminded himself.

With a smile—and feeling much more comfortable—he went on.

"I was reading your LinkedIn profile and noticed that you manage the youth basketball league with my aunt's best friend, Shayne Giorno. He's the one that encouraged me to talk to you in the first place."

"Shayne!" Lloyd laughed. "That guy's crazy. He and I played basketball in high school. Imagine my surprise when I saw him at your aunt's first barbecue!"

Bret laughed, feeling good that they had someone in common besides his aunt Maryam.

Taking advantage of the momentum, Bret kept things rolling. But he knew he couldn't just jump into a discussion, so he gave Lloyd a lead-up.

"What I'd like to do, Lloyd, is share some of my background

and situation. Then if it's okay, I have a couple of follow-up questions to get your perspective on."

Lloyd nodded. Bret took a relaxing breath and continued.

"As you know, I left the army after eight years. I earned two software engineering certificates during that time. Computers are great, but I think I'm interested in using my software education someplace where I feel I'm making a difference. Like for schools, or the medical field. But I'm open to anything that helps others and helps me grow."

Lloyd nodded thoughtfully, reflecting on what Bret said. Bret added, "And I just want to be clear, Lloyd: I'm not asking you to find me a job. I'm just trying to familiarize myself with the territory." This is where his research came into play. "For instance, could you tell me more about your company's product lines? I've done some reading, and I know you make audio components for other businesses. Do you see one sector growing faster than another? Are there changes or trends that might change the types of companies that I should be connecting with?"

Bret could see it: This question caused a change in Lloyd's expression. Something clicked, and ideas were forming in his mind.

Lloyd told Bret what he knew. He mentioned that a couple of their company partners seemed to be taking a new direction, while others were expanding their current efforts.

For Bret, this was a major eye-opener. Such changes meant they could be hiring. He wrote down the information making sure not to miss a single thing.

The conversation transitioned into his qualifications, and after a brief discussion about an industry certification course, Bret built up his courage to ask Lloyd about his own job search experience. After all, what better person to ask about the journey than someone who had already traveled the road?

"Last time we saw each other, Lloyd, you mentioned being in

my position at this time last year. To be honest, I've been having a tough time, and I'd appreciate hearing a thing or two you know now, that you wish you'd known then. If you'd be willing to share."

Again, Lloyd nodded. Bret was asking questions that he *himself* should have asked during his job search. Had he done so, he knew he would have had a much easier time finding work last year.

"You bet," Lloyd said simply. He sat forward on his seat. "The biggest thing: it was a domino effect. One thing led to another." He picked up his coffee. "I'm not proud to admit this, you understand, but it took me 'til last year to start networking. I should have been doing it my whole career—even when I was in the service. That's why last year was so bad for me: I hadn't been meeting new people. And it takes time to do that, and to get on calendars. That, plus I hadn't been in touch with people I already knew, including my old army buddies, which put me further behind. But once I started networking, I realized that it was nice to see old friends and colleagues again. We caught up. I learned new, important things about my field. And *that* made me understand more about what I was looking for. And *that* helped me understand who else I needed to network with. It really woke me up. And in my case, it brought me full circle. Truth is, had I talked with your aunt first, or even been in touch after I left the company, I might have gotten here sooner. Maybe you can see what I mean about the domino effect."

Bret nodded. He could. He could also see why meeting first with people he knew might be a good idea. And it was all making him feel much, much better. There were two decades between he and Lloyd, but this sounded just like his story.

Now that they were talking about it, Bret felt relieved that he hadn't let too much time get away from him before networking.

After all, if Lloyd, an experienced veteran and personable professional, had a tough time getting a job without networking, Bret was sure it would be even more difficult for him.

"Did networking do other things for you?" Bret asked, feeling braver now. "I mean besides, you know, seeing friends and helping get you a job?"

"Well, for starters, I have *new* friendships," Lloyd replied. "And yes, it's helped my day-to-day work because after meeting so many new people, I've developed a wide network that I use for business and a variety of other things. Sales for our products. New business development that leads to referrals. New business relationships for future partnerships. Even vacation suggestions."

Bret laughed. All good points, and all pearls of wisdom. Wisdom that was really common sense.

Wanting to keep things on track, Bret moved on to his next question. It was the toughest of them all, but he reminded himself of what Lloyd said about getting out there.

"You said you developed a wide network," Bret said. "That you kept meeting new people. I'm hoping to do the same—develop a wide network. Do you know others I could connect with as part of my job search? Maybe engineers or professionals connected to the education or medical world?"

Bret braced for the worst. He knew Lloyd was willing to lend advice, but Bret wasn't convinced that he would share names or think he was ready for additional meetings yet. But his question was coming from a place of sincerity. He could only be gracious if he was denied.

"I just might," Lloyd said. "There are a couple of vets from the event a few weeks back that work in those industries. Maybe a couple of people around here, too. I'm not sure if any are going to lead you right to a job, but they know other people, and they know people, too, so— maybe it's a start." Lloyd grinned and wrote a few names on a piece of paper.

"Is it all right that I use your name?" Bret asked.

"Yes, but just know that I'm still getting to know my co-workers here—I'm still kinda new, you understand. But I trust you, Bret, and I know you'll be prepared for them."

Bret thanked him and began putting his things back into his portfolio. He was done. It felt good, and he was grateful for Lloyd's help; enough to be sure this wouldn't be one-sided.

"One more question, Lloyd. How can I help *you*?"

Lloyd sat quietly. He had never been asked this before.

"I can't think of anything, Bret," he chuckled. "I kinda wasn't expecting that question!"

"Well, please think about it," Bret replied. "You're active with youth basketball. Two guys from my unit played in college and now coach kids. Maybe I can help there." He stood and held out his hand. "Or perhaps I can take you to lunch after I've landed a job."

"Where you going?" Lloyd asked as he stood and shook Bret's hand. Bret had said only twenty minutes, but *everyone* said that.

"A promise is a promise," Bret said. "I really appreciate your insights and your referrals, but I mean to let you get back to your day. Plus—I've got lots to do, too!"

Lloyd let go of Bret's hand and walked around the table. He was impressed with the way Bret carried himself and this meeting.

"Well, I'm glad I could help. I think we covered some good ground."

"Before I go," Bret said, opening his bag. "I wanted to give this to you as a token of thanks." It was a copied magazine article about hunting dogs. "The last time I saw you, I remember you mentioning dog training. I happened to read this article, and thought you might like what the author has to say."

Lloyd beamed as he thumbed through the article. It was a big expression of thanks, especially since he hadn't expected anything at all. More impressive was that Bret had remembered something that was dear to Lloyd—sporting dogs had been part of his family for generations.

"It's very thoughtful of you, Bret. Thank you!"

Lloyd's smile told Bret everything he needed to know about this meeting. It had gone right, and he had done a good job, even in spite of his reservations. It meant that with some practice, he could do this over and over again. Things were looking up.

"Thanks again for your time, Lloyd. I'll be in touch again after I've met with your colleagues. Have a good day!"

Q&A with Bret Abrams: "How did it go for you?"

What did you do to plan for your *20-Minute Networking Meeting*?
I looked Lloyd up on LinkedIn and was surprised by some things I didn't know about him. Like being connected to my aunt's friend, Shayne, through youth basketball. When I asked Shayne about it, he encouraged me to reach out. It was a coincidence running into Lloyd at the alumni event, as Lloyd had moved after getting a new job. But I felt my earlier homework had prepared me for the chance meeting.

How did the meeting itself go for you?
I liked it. I liked knowing that I felt respected for staying on track, too. In a way, Lloyd seemed to really respect that I was keeping to my word. Better yet, I got all the information I needed to continue my networking, and I have a feeling of optimism that I can do this networking thing.

Was twenty minutes long enough?
Definitely. Lloyd was actually the person asking for more time! I was still able to tell him about my background and what I was looking for. In that time, we were also able to cover a couple of other topics including his thoughts on networking.

What do you think Lloyd got out of it?
A new respect for me. I can be pretty introverted, and he saw a different me. Plus he's been in this position; I know that he knows it's hard. Seeing that I was willing to ask for help was a big deal. Also, before the meeting, I think Lloyd probably thought I wanted to get a job just anywhere. Telling him I was interested in something that would help others and help me grow was probably something he didn't know. It was good to clarify that point. It gives direction to my search, and helps me avoid accepting a job just for the sake of getting a job.

How do you plan to follow up?
I plan to send Lloyd an email today, thanking him for his time. I might also reiterate my willingness to help with youth basketball. I'll definitely let him know when I've made contact with the people he referred me to. He should know that I took advantage of what he offered me, and that I didn't waste his twenty minutes.

Is there anything you would do differently next time?
I'll stay more open about these meetings. I won't be as nervous. Only good things can come out of them—definitely nothing bad. At the very worst, nothing will happen at all.

Q&A with Lloyd Timmins: "How did it go for you?"

What did you like about Bret's *20-Minute Networking Meeting*?

Bret and I have known each other for awhile, but I like that he was still sensitive about my time. So many networking meetings are just long social sessions that don't get to the point. Maybe it's because it feels good to be in something like a business meeting, I don't know. But that's no excuse for disrespecting the time of others, and Bret didn't do that.

He also had things to talk about. He was prepared with things to discuss, and he knew a lot about my company. And he treated the meeting seriously; it wasn't just for chitchat, which could have been easy to do, considering how we know each other. He had thought ahead of time about what I could add to his job search, and he had some good questions lined up. I liked that. Plus, he brought me an article about dogs. That was not necessary, but thoughtful. I can't believe he remembered that conversation. Now I'll remember that he remembered.

Was it long enough?

Actually, not quite. I was literally left wanting more. I would have enjoyed talking to him for longer, but I know he's serious about his job hunt and has a lot to get done. If he gets back to me about how his meetings go with the people I set him up with, we'll probably get more time to catch up. Besides, I'm going to forward his information to another guy I know. We'll probably end up talking about that, too.

Were you expecting anything that didn't happen in this meeting?

I was expecting it to be longer and less structured. Networking meetings seem to be conversations where people want to just chat—a get-to-know-you session. This was different, and it threw me, but in a good way. Bret had a plan, which he stuck to, and he actually led the meeting. That was a first. I was surprised that all I had to do was sit back and help when I could. Which is the whole point, I suppose. Now I've learned something, too.

Is there anything you would change about the meeting?

Nothing about this meeting, in particular. But, I suppose there could be flexibility at times. If I was meeting with a friend or former co-worker that I had not seen in years, we might need more than twenty minutes to catch up. On the other hand, I suppose the catching up part is separate.

The End

You now have all the tools necessary for a new—and different—kind of job search. Take time to hone them. Make them yours. While the intent was to create a simple and straightforward model incorporating the best of what we have seen in the most effective networking meetings, it will be up to you to personalize your style and make things work in your favor. All it takes is the commitment and desire to make it happen.

As we part ways (for now), here are a few things to remember.

- **Networking is more than important. It is vital.** It is the life-blood of your job search and, in the big picture, your career.
- **Networking meetings don't have to be complicated.** Your simple objectives for each meeting are to learn a little, gain an additional contact or two, and hopefully, create an evangelist. If it doesn't happen in one meeting, don't dwell on it. Modify what needs to be changed and try to make it happen at the next. Remember, networking is a skill that can be *learned* and perfected with practice.

- **Networking meetings, like *any* meeting, have a beginning, middle, and end.** Remember that since you called the meeting, it will be up to you to manage where it stands. Be clear about the start, and once you've finished your brief and meaningful discussion, be clear about the end.

- **Throughout each of your discussions, you will be displaying your preparedness,** your organizational skills, your focus, and your genuine interest in the other person. Make it count. How well you do this will define the impression that you leave your contact with.

- **Networking is give-and-take!** Reciprocate, and always be prepared with something to give back.

- **Last but not least, *you have flexibility.*** I was careful to mention throughout the book that 20 minutes is merely a guideline. Networking, after all, is a people activity. Things jump off agenda, and topics take turns. This can be a good thing, as side-tracked conversation can lead to more information and more familiarity, which in turn strengthens your networking relationships. But remember to use judgment. If you get the sense that your meeting has strayed from the focus of your objectives, just get back on track!

That's it. *Fin! Finito!* The world is now your oyster. Take it. Own it. Make it yours!

We wish you the best as you hit the networking circuit and hope that your new experiences show immediate and permanent changes to your career objectives. Have faith. And trust. Without a doubt, positive change will come, and with it, the next solid step in your career!

APPENDIX

Your 20-Minute Networking Meeting Cheat Sheet

Print or tear this page out. Mark it. Use it as a guideline. Pace your house and be sure you know its order and its content. Once you have it locked down, figure out where there can be flexibility, and allow yourself to develop it.

Congratulations on finishing *The 20-Minute Networking Meeting*. Now go get started!

STEP 1:	Great First Impression
TIME LIMIT:	*2–3 minutes: thanks and chitchat*
STEP 2:	Great Overview
TIME LIMIT:	*1 minute overview of experience*
STEP 3:	Great Discussion
TIME LIMIT:	*12–15 minutes: 5 key questions*
STEP 4:	Great Ending
TIME LIMIT:	*2 minutes: thanks and wrap-up*
STEP 5:	Great Follow-Up
TIME LIMIT:	*Meaningful follow-up, right after the meeting*

The Readiness Exercise

(Or: Take This Little Test to See If You're Ready)

T ake twenty minutes to answer the following questions. Think through each answer before you write. This is not a race. It's about bringing focus to what you don't know about yourself yet. The purpose is to help you get grounded in what you bring to the market and to each networking interaction. These questions can be used as an indicator of your readiness to get into the job market. Don't stop here, however. You can continue to learn the steps of your *20-Minute Networking Meeting*, but be sure you have solid answers to the following questions before you begin any actual networking. Good luck!

The Readiness Exercise

1. What aspects of your work are you really, really good at? For guidance: What gets you the most compliments? What do you do faster, better than others?

_____

_____

_____

_____

2. What personality traits do you bring to the workplace? What characteristics have been praised by others? (i.e. efficient; innovative; strategic; communicative; adaptable; etc.) What aspects of your style have been particularly valued?

Now is probably a great time to dust off any personality or leadership-style inventories or assessments you may have taken in the past (such as Myers-Briggs or StrengthsFinder). If you don't have a recent assessment, it would be a good idea to take one or more now. Alternatively, you could ask some of your contacts for their perspective on this question. These might include family, friends, family friends, or former classmates, to name a few. (*Don't be afraid to ask. They'll see that you're doing the kind of homework that you should be doing.*)

_____

_____

_____

_____

3. What areas of specific expertise do you have that others don't? (Even if you don't have a lot of professional experience, think of what separates you from others who have the same or similar experience that you have.)

_____

_____

_____

_____

4. What else makes you a unique job candidate? (International experience; special training or certifications; early professional experience; languages; recognizable programs or group memberships; etc.)

_____

_____

_____

_____

5. Complete the following sentence:

"An organization would be fortunate to have me join them as

*(job role)*_____

because _____

_____

_____

_____

_____."

6. Respond to the following sentence: "Even though the above is true, I am still working on developing myself in the following areas." (This is where the perspectives of your contacts in Question 2 come in handy.) _____

_____

_____

_____

_____

_____

_____

_____

7. I am highly confident and ready going into my job search.
☐ Yes   ☐ No

8. I have the resources (Internet access; money for buses/trains; fees; resumes copies; etc.) to make my job search a great experience.
☐ Yes   ☐ No

DONE. Now take a ten-minute break and review your answers. Do they reflect what you *really* think and feel? Being sure you are rock-solid with these answers is what's going to give you confidence in your networking meetings. Don't rush it. And come back to this worksheet to revise your answers as you find a better way to express yourself.

The Great First Impression Planner

Here's a quick worksheet to help you figure out your game plan and how to make a solid first impression. Feel free to tear this out and fill it in if that's best for you.

WHAT YOU'RE GOING TO DO:

Take twenty minutes to answer these questions after setting up a meeting. Recheck your responses for any opportunity to tweak the answers or strengthen your information.

- **Arrival** *(Early, but not **too** early!)*
- **Where are we meeting?** *(Make sure this is established.)*
- **What's the address?** *(Make sure you're sure.)*
- **Do I know how to get there?** *(Be darned positive. You don't want to be late due to construction, weather, traffic, location parking, flat tire, or the odd traffic ticket.)*

FIRST IMPRESSIONS

If meeting at the contact's office, do I know the dress code, if any?

☐ Yes ☐ No

(**NOTE:** *If in doubt, ask a colleague or someone at the office's front desk. It's not a bad question to ask. Better yet, come dressed professionally. If you're a jobseeker, the last impression you want to leave is that you were more casually dressed than your contact.)*

Do I know how to pronounce the contact's name correctly?

☐ Yes ☐ No

(Boy, do we see and hear this one a lot. It's hard to help someone who doesn't even know your name. It's also hard to get past the embarrassment when you screw it up.)

SETTING THE AGENDA

Have you planned your agenda?

☐ Yes ☐ No

Do you know your five key questions? (Go back to *Step 3 — Great Discussion* if you don't recall this part.)

☐ Yes ☐ No

HIGHLIGHTING CONNECTIONS

Have I done my research in order to make great connections?

☐ Read the contact's company website.

☐ Read any personal bios available on the organization's website.

☐ Reviewed contact's LinkedIn profile; noted any connections in common.

☐ Did a Google search; noted any outside board positions; interests; things in common; etc.

☐ Jotted down key connections to mention in your *20-Minute Networking Meeting*.

The One-Minute Overview Planner

Okay, here's how you put together your one-minute overview.

WHAT TO DO:

- **Print a copy of your resume**
- **Decide what stands out**
- **Mark or highlight those items** (You'll be highlighting the most important features of your background that make you unique, as we've explained them in Step 2 - Great Overview.)
- **Find five to ten things in total** (Shoot for five at the very least.) Here are some possibilities:
  - Your current position, if you're in one now. If not, include trade school, classes or professional programs if you're in any.
  - Size and scope of your current responsibilities
  - Your prior position or positions, summarized, if you've had them
  - Your education and special certifications

NOTE: This list is meant to *complement* Step 2 — Great Overview, not replace it. Use that Chapter to build your Great Overview, and use this list to augment it.

WHAT TO DO NEXT:

- Compile these key points on another document
- Read through the points out loud
- Time it. If it takes around one minute out loud, perfect; you've got your one-minute overview. If you're over, trim the fat and keep the most important points.
- If you're too short of a minute, add another point or leave it as-is if you feel good about it
- Finally, string it all together using your own words (Also known as "making it yours"). Take your time. Make it fluid and easy to understand. Done.

A QUICK REVIEW

Here, reworded, is the structure for your One-Minute Overview:

- Think about your number of years in the function / Industry
- Combine with the highlights of your background / Highlight awards or achievements unique to you
- Follow with the places you've worked / Professional Experiences you've had or will have
- Tie them in with the most recent titles you've held / Or focus on what you intend to do with the experience you already have

Now string them all together in a sentence or two (three or more will work, too—just stick with one minute). *Voilà!* One-minute overview!

Your Small Token
of Gratitude

(Actual Things You Can Give in Return)

The consummate giver in my own network is our colleague Lars, a man who is 100% focused, 24/7, on what he can give to others. He has been cited as the "Most Networked Person in the Twin Cities" by the publication *Minnesota Business*. Lars is mid-30s and the most networked person because other people like knowing him. And they like knowing him because he is a giver at all levels.

Lars shared his philosophy of *giving* as a strategy for jobseekers. Here is a thank-you note that he received (printed with his permission, with names changed to protect anonymity):

Hi, Lars:

I accepted a position at XYZ Corporation and start my new job on Monday! You can read the story in the business publication, but basically I'll be running their national sales and operations. It's a tremendously exciting opportu-

nity and I'm just thrilled (and they are pretty happy, too).

I wanted to send you a heartfelt letter of thanks. You were perhaps the most influential person in my search, which found its true spark when we had coffee together. The idea of using this time to give back was the thesis statement of the last four months. I met more people, had more interesting meetings, made more of a difference, and was happier and more satisfied because of that advice.

My life has been measurably improved and it came from that simple thought: Don't think of what your network can do for you, think about what you can do for your network. And you were the person who sparked that idea, so I owe you a big thank-you.

Signed,
Executive Candidate

There you have it. Giving back will work wonders for you, too.

Here are a few things you can give your contact in return. It never has to be anything big—just something that shows your appreciation.

- **Contact names.** This is a great one. Think about people in your own network that your contact might want to meet, and offer to make introductions.
  NOTE: Remember that *every* person you know is a contact. Finding common ground between two people is the connector. You have more of a network than you realize!

- **Information.** Find up-to-date information on your contact's industry or functional area. If your research uncovers this person's hobbies or interests (such as animal rights, environmentalism, or the clarinet), take related contacts, connections, articles, websites, etc., to the meeting.

- **Potential client ideas.** If the person is a consultant, or related in any way to sales or marketing, he or she would likely be very appreciative of any ideas or referrals that you might have for possible clients. Even if your referral doesn't pan out in a sale, trust me, it will be appreciated.

- **An actual gift.** We understand that not everyone has budget room to spend on gifts, but there are inexpensive alternatives, too. Perhaps a gift card to a coffee chain for an especially helpful contact. Maybe some chocolates. We've seen everything from restaurant gift cards and children's toys (it's a long story) to decorative mini-art pieces and invitations to interesting professional and cultural events.

⬦⬦⬦

TIP

Post-holiday sales can be a boon, as can purchasing items in bulk. One enterprising young networker showed his appreciation by sending me hand-tied fly fishing flies marked with which streams to use them on. If *you* have such arts and crafts experience, you could do this too and save yourself a lot of money! What if all else fails? Do a web search for great inexpensive gift ideas! (And never feel obligated to buy a trick pony or cruise tickets. *Nothing huge!*)

⬦⬦⬦

The Great Discussion Planner

This section is a summary of the five key questions. Using it, take twenty minutes to plan a great discussion, and use it as a quick reference for future conversations.

QUESTIONS 1–3
(THREE UNIQUE QUESTIONS)

Think about what you know about this networking contact. What information is this person uniquely able to give you? The questions are structured as follows:

> **Fact about Contact (Observation)**
> *followed by*
> **Follow-Up Question (Related Question)**

Here are the breakdowns followed by their full approach:

KEY QUESTION - EXAMPLE 1:

Fact about Contact (Observation):
Your law firm, Simon & Schim, was recently acquired by a much larger house.

Follow-Up Question (Related Question):
What was your experience in the merger process?

FULL APPROACH:

"Your law firm, Simon & Schim, was recently acquired by a much larger house. What was your experience in the merger process?"

KEY QUESTION - EXAMPLE 2:

Fact about Contact (Observation):
You participated in an international nursing exchange program.

Follow-Up Question (Related Question):
How did that help develop your career? Is it a good idea for someone of my experience?

FULL APPROACH:

"You participated in an international nursing exchange program. How did that help develop your career? Is it a good idea for someone of my experience?"

KEY QUESTION - EXAMPLE 3:

Fact About Contact (Observation):
You are a graduate of the Automation Machinists School.

Follow-Up Question (Related Question):
Was that the best way to kick-start your career? In what way?

FULL APPROACH:

"You graduated from the Automation Machinists School. Was that the best way to kick-start your career? In what way?"

YOUR TURN—QUESTIONS 1–3

Observation: _____

Related Question: _____

Observation: _____

Related Question: _____

Observation: _____

Related Question: _____

QUESTION 4: OTHER CONTACTS

You can use the following question exactly as written, or modify it slightly to your style. No matter how you phrase it, you must ask for additional referrals.

"Is there someone else you know (from your trade group; Chamber; industry organization; current company; alumni association, etc.) that I might talk with as I network?"

Your Turn — Question 4 _____

QUESTION 5: HOW CAN I HELP YOU?

Again, you can use the following question exactly as written, or modify it slightly to your style. No matter how you phrase it, just *be sure to ask* how you can help in return.

"You have been so helpful to me. How can I help **you**?*"*

Your Turn — Question 5 _____

The Great
Follow-Up Tracker

WHAT TO DO

Take twenty minutes to follow up after each networking meeting. Here are the steps, laid out for you.

Contact name _____

Business _____

Date _____

FOLLOW UP WITH THE NETWORKING CONTACT

1. Send a brief thank-you to the networking contact.
   ☐ Done
2. Send a brief thank-you to the person who referred you to that contact.
   ☐ Done
3. Add any new or updated information about this person to your networking database.
   ☐ Done

4. Make a note to follow up with this contact, as appropriate.

☐ Done

FOLLOW UP WITH YOURSELF

1. What did you do well?_____

_____

_____

2. What will you do differently next time? _____

_____

_____

3. What did you learn and how will you apply that information?

_____

_____

_____

FOLLOW UP WITH NEW CONTACTS

1. What names of future contacts did you get?

_____

_____

2. Schedule follow-up with each of these new contacts.

☐ Done

About the Authors

NATHAN A. PEREZ is Principal at 20-Minute Communications, LLC., a consultancy that helps all experience levels of job-seekers from across the country. He is a national speaker on the topics of networking, resume deconstruction, and LinkedIn.

As part of his 20-Minute Communications consultancy, Nathan continues to work in executive search in the Research function. Responsible for the first step in the executive recruitment process, Nathan devises the strategies of "where and how to find" qualified candidates for client companies. He has been cited by *The Huffington Post* as one of the most connected people on LinkedIn world-wide.

Co-author of the acclaimed job-search networking book *The 20-Minute Networking Meeting,* Nathan teaches its 5 principles to students, career coaches and executives. An enthusiastic and hands-on coach, Nathan helps strengthen the presence of his job-searching clients by combining his executive search experience with 20 years in front of television cameras and stage performance. A formally trained actor, Nathan spent 20 years in New York City and Hollywood as a professional performer and writer. He is a member of the Actors Equity Association union (AEA), and a voting union member of The Screen-Actors Guild (SAG-AFTRA).

He lives in Minneapolis with his wife and two kids. You can get in touch or read more about him at www.20mnm.com.

MARCIA BALLINGER is a Co-Founder and Principal at Ballinger|Leafblad, a St. Paul-based executive search firm focused on serving the civic sector. She conducts executive search projects for top executives in non-profit organizations, higher education, foundations and professional associations. A frequent presenter to groups of executives, Marcia is widely known as a no-nonsense representative of the executive search industry.

Marcia has a BS in Business Administration and an MA in Speech-Communication along with a PhD in Organization and Management from Capella University where she now serves on the Board of Directors. She was named an Industry Leader by the Minneapolis/St. Paul Business Journal in 2008.

A resident of St. Paul, Marcia lives with her husband Brad, daughter Analisa and their two French Bulldogs. She is at work on a new book focused on job interviewing skills.